Suffering: A Test of Theological Method

Suffering: A Test of Theological Method

ARTHUR C. McGILL

Foreword by
Paul Ramsey and William F. May

THE WESTMINSTER PRESS
Philadelphia

Acknowledgment is made to the following for permission to reprint their copyrighted material:

Cambridge University Press and Oxford University Press, for quotations from *The New English Bible, New Testament.* © The Delegates of the Oxford University Press and The Syndics of the Cambridge University Press 1961.

Alfred A. Knopf, Inc., for a quotation from *The Plague*, by Albert Camus, copyright 1948 by Stuart Gilbert.

The Macmillan Company, for a quotation from *Prisoner for God: Letters and Papers from Prison*, by Dietrich Bonhoeffer, copyright 1953 by The Macmillan Company.

National Council of Churches, Division of Christian Education, for Scripture quotations from the Revised Standard Version of the Bible, copyright 1946 and 1952.

Charles Scribner's Sons, for a quotation from *Jesus Christ and Mythology*, by Rudolf Bultmann, copyright © 1958 Rudolf Bultmann.

The Westminster Press, for quotations from *Christology of the Later Fathers*, The Library of Christian Classics, Vol. III, ed. by Edward R. Hardy. Published in the U.S.A. by The Westminster Press, 1954.

Published by The Westminster Press®
Philadelphia, Pennsylvania

PRINTED IN THE UNITED STATES OF AMERICA
9 8 7 6 5 4 3 2 1

Library of Congress Cataloging in Publication Data

McGill, Arthur Chute.
  Suffering : a test of theological method.

  1. Suffering—Religious aspects—Christianity.
2. Theology. I. Title.
BT732.7.M28   231'.8   82-6934
ISBN 0-664-24448-3 (pbk.)   AACR2

Contents

Foreword

A DISTINGUISHED philosopher and theologian from England once wrote that Arthur C. McGill was the only person he met in the course of his long stay in this country who had the chance of becoming for his generation what Paul Tillich and Reinhold Niebuhr were to theirs. No one knew better than Professor McGill how uncontrollable and, in the long run, inconsequential such matters of eminence are. Those of us who knew him, however, reckoned with a brilliance, boldness, and clarity in his thought that prompts us to want to see the small portion of his work committed to print made accessible again. The little gem, SUFFERING: A TEST OF THEOLOGICAL METHOD, first published in 1968 and long out of print, is a case in point.

Suffering poses the fundamental test for theology in our time. How can one affirm the existence and powerfulness of God when men and women find themselves beset and stricken by powers that twist, violate, sicken, and destroy? Theology must reckon with this fundamental challenge to belief in God—not the challenge of academic atheism that treats the question of God's existence as a kind of intellectual puzzle, but a profoundly practical atheism born of the experience of suffering.

McGill's work on the subject received little attention in its day. But it has a continuing contribution to make, much greater than the popular books of the 60s that are now embarrassingly outdated. In the course of this brief book, McGill employs, unobtrusively but brilliantly, the categories furnished by the phenomenologists of religion to explore the raw human experience of suffering. He then unexpectedly revisits the ancient debate over the doctrine of the Trinity to throw light on the understanding of God which the experience of suffering raises. And he closes with tantalizing implications for Christian ethics, especially for ethics on the American scene.

Recall that McGill's book came out just three years after the publication of *The Secular City*. That book, along with its many variants and derivatives, affirmed and celebrated human autonomy and control over a world that was secular, and secular without significant remainder. McGill disputes the Bonhoeffer/Cox diagnostic thesis in his crucial chapter on "Demonism—The Spiritual Reality of Our Day." The modern world, for better or for worse, reeks of religion. This religion, however, hardly derives from the official, Biblical religion of the West, with its notion of a creative, nurturant, and preservative God. On the contrary, modern men and women are given to the pervasive conviction that the world and its inhabitants are in the grip of dominative, abusive, and destructive powers. Legendary associations aside, the modern spiritual experience remains at its core largely what the New Testament identifies as the demonic.

In developing this thesis, McGill relies (without troubling his readers with the scholarly details) on the categories furnished by Van der Leeuw and others among the great students of religion. The gods, argued Van der Leeuw, are relative latecomers in the history of religion. Long before the emergence of modern, official religious traditions and their developed (and somewhat tame) theologies, religion consisted of some sort of experience of sacred power. Powerfulness characterized the object of religion; and awe, dread, alertness, or attentiveness characterized the religious subject before this object. Western piety fixed its attentiveness upon a creative, nurturant, and preservative God; and modern celebrators of secularity have vested this powerfulness in the human capacity for command and control. The lived experience of our time, however, differs from the hymns of conventional theists or secular humanists.

McGill seeks his evidence for the religious preoccupations of our time not in the pessimistic works of a cultural elite, the eccentric few—Melville, Joyce, Eliot, Frost, or Stevens, whose writings he knew well—but rather in the daily newspapers. The mass media blurt out daily and relentlessly what commands our attention, what we find truly newsworthy, what has sufficient energy and allure to deserve our alertness. The contents of the front page make it ringingly clear that the perceived powers active in our midst are violent and destructive—heart attacks, war, crime, corruption, cancer, tornados, delinquency, runaway social problems, impersonal and threatening economic forces that are largely on the move and out of control.

The very format of the headline slug and the television

news story emphasizes eruptive, invasive forces that over-take the everyday world by surprise. Far from the serene picture offered by secular science of a world pliant to explanation, prediction, and human intervention, men and women experience themselves as relatively helpless victims, buffeted and battered by largely arbitrary, destructive power. And even when the society mobilizes forces to resist destructive power (as in the case of disease and war), it finds that the resistance itself has its destructive side effects. "Iatrogenic illness," as it is currently called in the field of medicine, heralds the destructive side effects of the very effort to heal and cure. Thus men and women largely appear to be passive victims rather than agents, sufferers rather than actors, on the human scene.

If demonism constitutes the dominant religious experience of our time, then suffering poses the central theological problem. In attempting to wrestle theologically with the problem, McGill has to rethink first the anthropological presupposition of suffering. Suffering can occur only because men and women are not self-sufficient monads. They are characterized by neediness. They are vulnerable to external powers that support and threaten them.

Response to this neediness can take two basic forms. In the first instance, men and women can attempt to secure themselves against exigency by establishing a circle of possessions that support and protect them from threat. They can attempt to free themselves from the threat of domination by dominating their environment. They can never do so perfectly, of course, because they remain vulnerable and hostage to the blows of disease, accident, fate, and death. Thus they find themselves possessed both by their possessions and by those powers that threaten to dispossess them. This is the strategy of the closed self, which increases suffering even while it would seek to escape it.

Second, the self may conceivably open out toward others in a self-giving, self-expending, donative love. This is the response of the open self—openhanded rather than tightfisted—the identity that Leo Tolstoy and Gabriel Marcel, in their differing ways, described and commended. Such an identity is not an abstract possibility. Jesus, preeminently and unconditionally, lived it out under the concrete conditions in which people find themselves buffeted by destructive power. He suffered dreadful pain, isolation, betrayal, abandonment, and death, but his identity with self-expending love never broke. This is the identity which Christians celebrate in worship and share in love.

The key theological question, however, remains. What connection does this identity have with the divine being? Is Jesus' self-expending love itself a definition of the divine powerfulness? Or is God's power yet another kind of powerfulness beyond Jesus? If God is other than the power disclosed in Jesus, then the ultimacy of what men and women reckon with in Jesus is compromised. McGill's reflection on suffering reaches its climax in the chapter on the Trinity. "Self-giving as the Inner Life of God" may be the boldest essay written on that baffling subject in the twentieth century. Except for Karl Barth and a few others, most modern theologians have shown little interest in the question of the inner life of God, and lay people even less. The doctrine of the Trinity has seemed little more than a numbers game: Is God one or somehow one in three? But McGill revisits the fourth-century controversy between the theologians Arius and Athanasius and sees therein a religiously crucial struggle over one's understanding of the divine powerfulness.

One concept of divine power, we have already seen, derives from the experience of the demonic—power associated with the power to dominate, the power that beleaguered men and women dream about and that they ordinarily impute to the divine when they refer to God's almightiness. The ascription usually refers to God's power to dominate absolutely. So conceived, God is absolutely self-enclosed, self-sufficient, and transcendent, beholden to none. This was Arius' conception of powerfulness and, given this conception, he could not affirm Jesus Christ as equal to God, of one substance with God. Jesus, after all, received all things from the Father. He was needy with respect to the Father; therefore, of a certainty he must be inferior to the Father, a creature somewhere above us, to be sure, but far short of divine. To be divine is to be the Super-dominator of all things, beholden to none. This vision of power fits in, of course, with the politics of the late Roman Empire, which makes it quite natural to think of God on the model of a remote, relatively inaccessible emperor, and of Jesus Christ as an intermediate lieutenant or chieftain, somewhere between the emperor and the ordinary run of men and women. But more than that, the Arian vision fits in with notions of demonic power—in any time or any place.

Athanasius and the church, so argues McGill, had to insist that the Son was equal to the Father, true God from true God, not for the petty reasons of number or rank, but in order to defend and preserve its very different vision of the divine powerfulness. It discovered in Jesus the powerfulness of self-communicating love. That love which it discovered in Jesus was not subordinate to yet another power above it, the power to dominate, but is itself the ultimate. The two poles of that love in the divine life are giving and receiving, the Father and the Son. Without a recognition of the coequality of these two poles in the divine life, giving suddenly corrupts into something other than itself; that is, it deteriorates from a true and full self-communication into a subtle kind of domination that covertly controls through its giving. We know only too well this deception in the human sphere under the mode of the philanthropist—the one who in the self-sufficiency of his life gives to others and dominates them through his giving. His superiority rests on his freedom from neediness. The Christian faith, on the contrary, affirms, celebrates, and shares a power that is vibrantly itself, nurturant and needy, giving and receiving, Father and Son, in the unity of the Spirit.

The book closes with tantalizing leads into the subject of Christian ethics that follow directly from these reflections on the Trinity. Most American moralists truncate their understanding of love and reduce it to philanthropy when they emphasize the importance of giving but obscure the element of receiving in the moral life. The pretension of the philanthropist underlies the posture of the American nation, the American church, and the modern professional, both lay and Christian, whenever they position themselves as relatively self-sufficient givers, while others appear before them in their neediness. Thus in their powerfulness, the American nation gave to developing nations, the American churches to missions, conscientious lawyers to their clients, physicians to their patients, and teachers to their students, in the outward procession of philanthropic love.

The dynamics of giving is central to Christian ethics, but that ethics betrays the power that nourishes it if it obscures the element of receiving in the Christian life. Christian ethics needs to recover both poles which the inner life of God itself reveals: giving and receiving. If love is the virtue appropriate to the pole of giving, then humility and gratitude are virtues appropriate to the pole of receiving in the moral life. Americans, the American church, and professionals in America are in particular need of this second emphasis as they fear to lose, in receiving from others, their position of dominance over them.

Given this vision, McGill's book rightly includes a meditation on the story of the good Samaritan. In its conventional reading, the story fits so tidily into the world of the philanthropist: it appears to divide humankind into the well-off and the needy and to accept responsibility for the latter. Christians must, indeed, love the needy (the story, after all, concludes, "Go and do likewise"): but, first and foremost, Christians must do so as those who know themselves to be the needy man on the side of the road. They are givers, to be sure, but not abstracted from their receiving.

That truth is hard to come by. It is better to give than to receive, but often it is more difficult to receive than to give. Arthur McGill moved in the direction of this truth in his book and he had to live it out in his life. Possessed of an abundance of energy, imagination, and intelligence, he was a brilliant teacher, whose students across twenty-nine years at Amherst College, Wesleyan University, Princeton University, and Harvard Divinity School received richly from his work. Despite the constant encroachment of a severe childhood-onset disease that eventually took his life in September 1980, he commanded the classroom absolutely. Some found that influence so great as to be troubling—too dominating. That troubled him in turn for, in fact, he received in the giving.

PAUL RAMSEY
WILLIAM F. MAY

Easter 1982

"I have said this to you, that in me you may have peace. In the world you have tribulation; but be of good cheer, I have overcome the world." (*John 16: 33.*)

"We must form our estimate of men less from their achievements and failures, and more from their sufferings."

—*Dietrich Bonhoeffer,*
Prisoner for God:
Letters and Papers from Prison.

1

Violence
and Theology

I N OUR modern world, violence seems to touch us on
every side. We meet it in the agony of war on the
international scene, in the rising rate of criminal violence in our cities, in the statistics on disease and insanity
from our hospitals. We experience it just in the intense
pace of everyday life. The husband who must commute,
the wife who must take her children to this appointment
or that affair, the pressure of endless details which require
tight schedules and much haste—all these put a special
strain on the human personality. Each individual tries to
handle and bear the violence of this pressure as best he
can. He may take tranquilizers or indulge in hobbies or
seek escape in reading. But the pressure is there and he
finds himself, to some extent, living on nerves.

The term "violence" refers to an event or an action
that "violates" some aspect of human life. Violence,
then, is always connected with *suffering*. But not all suffering involves the quality of violence. The pain of guilt
that a person feels may be so deep and may spread
through his awareness so gradually that no force of
"violence" is detectable.

What the word "violence" points to is the element of intensity in an experience of suffering. Violence may designate the *intensity of power* in the action that causes the suffering, as when we speak of a man's violent temper or the sun's violent light or the violence of Hitler's persecutions.

But the word may also be used to refer to the *intensity of pain* that such power causes: a violent headache, a violent dread of fire. Whenever suffering is caused by an excessive application of power and therefore gives a person the experience of being twisted or crushed by that power, we have an instance of violence.

Every age has a peculiar kind of evil to which it is especially sensitive. Here it feels that the full sinfulness of evil is most starkly exhibited. Whenever it wants to confront the misery and negative side of life, then it tends to consider examples of this kind of evil. Certain primitive groups focus on the experience of debility, or the wasting away of human vitality through age or sickness or folly. They find the most terrible depths of evil made visible in this kind of experience. However, the people of Victorian England one hundred years ago seem to have been gripped by the evil of human immorality, by the flaws in a person's character, or by the weaknesses in his will.

Our age seems to be obsessed with the suffering caused by violence. People today are moved with compassion for those who are weak, and are greatly troubled by those who are immoral. Yet the uncertainties and ambiguities of right and wrong seem pale beside the horror of the concentration camps. In the spectacle of such monumental suffering the awfulness of life's ordeal is most truly revealed. There the issues of love and hate, of life and death, of hope and despair are encountered in their ultimate seriousness. There men confront what is antihuman in its most destructive form. There evil steps forth and shows its true paralyzing enormity. For our age violent suffering is not seen as just one of the many inevitabilities of life with which people must learn to live. It is felt to be *the scandal* that threatens to undermine all confidence in the decent values that make life possible. For this reason, no literary work or dramatic production, no cowboy television program or profound philosophical novel, seems able to claim our serious consideration today unless it stands in relation to an area of violence.

The Christian church understands itself by identification in some way with Jesus Christ. Furthermore, it sees Jesus Christ as, in some way, God's agent in the redemption of men, as the one through whom men are freed from evil and brought to the fullness of their existence. Of course, over the centuries Christians have suggested a great many ways of understanding how Christ brings about this redemption and how men other than Christ are able to benefit from his work. What is always recognized is that he liberates men, not from merely minor troubles or secondary problems, but from the worst and the ultimate evil. For people today such ultimate evil is embodied in the experience of violent suffering. Therefore, if Christ is the redeemer, as the Christian church believes, in what way does he redeem men from this terrible evil?

There is remarkably little said on this subject in Christian literature today. But for many Christians and for many atheists the problem of violent suffering is of decisive significance. In the face of such enormous suffering in the world, they ask, how can anyone believe in a good God who redeems men from evil? And if Christians do in fact believe in the power of this God, as they claim, why are they just as stunned, just as perplexed, and just as unnerved by violent suffering as everyone else? Christians may hold a fine code of decency as their ethic of love. They may even have an all-embracing principle of explanation in their doctrine of creation. But if they believe in Christ as the redeemer, why do they not live as if they had victory in the face of suffering? Precisely at this all-important point, say the atheists, precisely here where evil stands forth in its most terrible form, Christians become as frightened as everyone else and so belie their religious claims. Their God, it seems, proves to be inadequate or incompetent in the face of suffering.

The question to be explored in the following chapters is simply this: *What is the meaning of violent suffering in the sphere of Christ's redemption?*

THE TERMS OF OUR INQUIRY

Before beginning our investigation of this matter, a word is necessary regarding general procedures. In this inquiry we will be engaged in a work of Christian theology. We should therefore be alert to some of the features and pitfalls of such an undertaking.

First of all, Christian theology is disciplined and responsible thinking about God as revealed and worshiped in Jesus Christ. It is focused upon Christ as the power of

God and the wisdom of God. In their thinking, men may obviously consider all sorts of things besides God. And when they seek an understanding of God they may take other routes than the way of Jesus Christ. Even Jesus Christ himself may be approached in terms other than as the presence and revelation of God—for instance, as a man who shows historians the world of Palestine in the first century. But all thought that seeks an understanding of God in and through Jesus Christ is Christian theology.

Christian theologians, however, do not acquire contact with Christ by reaching out toward him with their mental faculties. Rather, they know him as one who affects and informs their concrete living, their own personal way of being. Even before they begin to think about the meaning of Christ, they are already in touch with him, already related to him and aware of him. If they seek to understand him, it is because in some sense they already know him.

What is this relation to Christ which precedes theology? It is the relation of a person who finds himself *turned toward Christ for life and light.* This "life" and this "light" must be more fully explained.

The life that Christ brings is not an improvement of the life men have naturally. It is not the vitality that they have, for instance, because they have been born, or because they are intelligent, or because they are caught up in the hopes and passions of some community. The life that Jesus brings is believed to be the *life of God himself.* Through Jesus, God gathers men into his own life. This is what the New Testament calls "eternal life." In that sense it is nothing else and nothing less than *him-*

self which God shares with men. Jesus calls upon men to give to one another what is most peculiarly theirs, what is most fully identical with themselves—namely, their very lives. They are to do this because this is the way God deals with them. God gives men a share in his eternal life, and therefore, as servants of this God, they should share such life as they possess with one another.

The "eternal life" that Jesus brings, then, is not just another form of ordinary life, which is somehow freed from death and made interminable. Rather, eternal life is a new and unique order of life, an elevation and transfiguration of the ordinary, a share in the divine life. That is why a person's turning to Jesus has been called a "birth," since it is believed to involve his entering a new life and not simply his enhancing the life that he already possesses. And because the new life is God's own, this birth makes him a "child of God" in a very precise sense. Now he is not only made by God, like other creatures, as a vase is made by the artisan, but he is made alive by God's own vitality, as a child is informed by the life of his parents. He is "born, not of blood nor of the will of the flesh nor of the will of man, but of God" (John 1: 13).

If the word "life" points to God's gift of himself in Christ, a gift that affects men within, the term "light" points to the outer blessing of this gift. Light at the sensory level is that which opens the world to us, that which removes the closedness, the hiddenness, the inaccessibility of things. Whatever stands in the dark remains alien and estranged from us. Jesus is spoken of as the light of the world (John 8: 12) whom the darkness cannot overcome (ch. 1: 5). These references suggest how, through Jesus, men are gathered into a realm of *un-obstructed openness* at every level, a realm where all hiding, all estrangement, and therefore all fear are removed. For instance, it is not necessary in this realm for a person to conceal some bit of himself from others, in order to have a secure identity which they will not take and abuse. He does not have to hide behind pretensions and self-justifications. Christ reveals God to be light as well as life, and to be *for us men* the light as well as the life. And because he is unreservedly open both in himself and toward us, those who live in relation to him may be unreservedly open to one another. They may put aside all lying, all hypocrisy, all desperate secrecy and deception. In Christ they find not only a principle of life that abolishes all death but also a principle of openness that dispels all darkness and closedness, all distrust and alienation.

By theologizing, even with the finest intellectual equipment, no man is able to bring himself into fruitful contact with Jesus as the power of God and the wisdom of God. No man can bring about his own birth into the divine life. Every theological investigation can only be undertaken by men who in their actual existence are already oriented toward Christ as the divine life and the divine light of men. *Theology always presupposes people who are Christians,* in the sense of living with this orientation.

Theology does have a very special role to play, however, for understanding is the faculty by which we humans participate in openness. A man's understanding is what enables him to see into other people and things, to bring them forth from their hiding. But understanding, especially through the power of speech, is also what enables him to open himself to other people and things. By their understanding, then, men participate in the light —in the openness—of God. Theology, as an activity of the understanding, represents a responsible effort to celebrate and share in the light of God, to gather the broken and clouded fragments of human existence into the radiant openness that Christ brings. That is why theology is not an activity restricted to experts. It is to be undertaken by everyone who knows Christ as the light of the world and who exercises his understanding to participate in that light and to share it with others.

From Darkness Toward Light

Theology presupposes an orientation to Christ as life and light. Having made this assertion, we must immediately say something further, for it is quite evident that, whatever their "orientation" may be, Christians do *not* in fact exist with a life completely free from death or in a realm completely free from alienation. On the contrary, all the torments and problems of life known to other men continue to be with them, though perhaps no longer enveloping them completely.

If the existence of Christians is oriented *toward* Christ as the life and light of God, it is in movement *away from* evil and death and darkness. In other words, the Christian is *on the way* from evil to good, from death to life, from darkness to light. He finds himself in a state of pilgrimage.

This means that he never knows the life and light of Christ simply by themselves. He knows them as a life and light that expose the death and darkness from which he comes. Christ not only reveals God but discloses the emptiness and dreadfulness of all life without God. Until God's openness comes, it is possible to be appreciative and grateful for any small superficial acts of self-opening on the part of people. Relative to the isolation and hiddenness in which men often live, these acts seem good. But when exposed by the light of God, when measured by the total openness that belongs to God's life, these acts turn out to be quite inadequate and to be, themselves, masks behind which people hide. How many impressive vitalities may be called "life," until they stand under God's aliveness and there have all their deficiencies and mortality fully exposed. Jesus, because he discloses the power and wisdom of God, also reveals the essential impotence and folly of life in this world apart from God. He burns the false securities away, shatters the false gods, displays the corruption in dreams of innocence and the tawdriness in most heroism.

We must say, then, that a man is not only led by Jesus Christ into a new life, but he is also led into a deeper awareness of the bankruptcy of his old life, of the scope and tenacity of the evil *from which* he is being taken. This is what is meant when Christian theologians speak of Christ as bringing to men both condemnation and justification, judgment and mercy, death and life. Christ reveals not only the richness of the goal toward which they move but also the sterility and horror of the state from which they move.

The Christian existence that theology presupposes is certainly one that is *being* oriented toward Christ as the life and light. It is also an existence that is *being* delivered from its bondage to death and estrangement, from its own folly and fear. An investigation by Christian theology, therefore, must not only be about this movement; it must reflect and be caught up within this movement. It must itself be in transition from darkness toward light. Jesus as the light of the world makes theology possible, because he orients the understanding toward a new principle of openness. But the fact that the Christian finds himself in transition makes theology necessary, for this means that he does not yet rest in the truth but must constantly be discovering it in the midst of his darkness.

A theological investigation can never be simply the application of ready-made, authoritative answers to human questions. It must be a real labor, moving always toward the light of Christ, but in that light wrestling with real darkness—with questions that truly dismay and perplex, questions that arise from the torments of existence, like the question of suffering.

This means that theology must avoid putting truth in some fixed formula which is supposed to be valid for all time, and which can never be qualified by the concrete problems of real existence. For men to remove the knowledge of God from their own actual movement from ignorance to knowledge, from obscurity to clarity, and from darkness to light is to lose the truth of God entirely. For God's light is only available to men now as that which takes them from the darkness again and again and again.

The darkness that threatens always has a very specific character, peculiar to each place and time. The estrangements and alienations that tempt people to withdraw and live in a closed way are quite different for an apartment dweller in Manhattan and for a native in the

Congo. Any theology that wrestles with a point of darkness will think and speak responsibly only if it grasps that darkness in its peculiar concreteness as the darkness that a man knows in his specific existence.

Yet even at this level of theological work, Jesus Christ is central. For he is not only the life and light of God in relation to men; he is also man subjected to evil and darkness and death. He is not only the goal of the Christian life; he is also the way toward that goal, the movement from alienation to openness, from death to life. Men do not have to leave their lost condition and progress toward God before they can be in contact with Christ. In Christ, God reaches all the way to them in their lostness. Christ enters the realm of their evil so as to draw them to himself.

Therefore, whenever Christians investigate a real question from their actual existence—and every serious question is a legitimate concern for them—they must not only formulate it in terms of their own lives in their own world. They must go on and learn about how this darkness figures in the existence of Jesus. They must carry their knowledge of both good and evil to him, and *into* him. Only in that way can they discover the real darkness in their own perplexity, and begin to be liberated from such false readings and misinterpretations of darkness as may characterize the pretensions of their age and their social class.

THEOLOGY AND SCRIPTURE

If the Christian in his existence and in his thought focuses on Christ, this is because Christ is present to him.

And Christ is present to him because of Holy Scripture.

A distinction is crucial at this point. The Bible is a vast literature, filled with all sorts of information and viewpoints. But above and beyond the various details that they contain, the Biblical documents mean to point —or witness—to Jesus Christ as the power and wisdom of God. The books of the Old Testament point in expectation and those of the New Testament point in fulfillment. For Christian theology the incomparable value of the Bible does not lie in this element of variety of detail, but in the witness of the various writers. As written in the Confession of 1967 of The United Presbyterian Church U.S.A., "the Scriptures are not a witness among others [to Jesus Christ], but the witness without parallel." It is not as a history book or as a scientific book or as a book of events or even as a record of man's religious beliefs that the theologian reads the Bible, but as a witness to Christ. The Scriptures function as a servant of their Lord. We are meant not to rest in them but to move through them and beyond them to the One they serve.

Theology is often tempted to rest in the words of Scripture and to read these books as if they transcribed God's life and light for man into words. But theology must resist this temptation. The Bible as such is not the light of the world; nor is the Bible as such the principle of openness which no darkness can overcome. In all its investigations theology must move beyond the Scriptural statements and seek to discern the form of Jesus Christ himself.

This is only another way of saying that the Bible must be *interpreted* in theological work. It is never enough simply to quote its words, because its words must be penetrated until they yield the reality of Christ to us in our concrete existence, as the one who bears our evil and gathers us into God's life and light.

THEOLOGY AND THE UNBELIEVER

There is one last consideration. What of the Christian's needy neighbors? What of the relation of theologizing to the unbelievers who hunger for life?

No theological investigation can be genuinely Christian which is not genuinely open to the unbeliever and which does not include the unbeliever within its probing efforts. For theology is not just a detached intellectual exercise about a certain subject matter. It itself is a participation in Christ's redemptive work. It itself is an event in which some bit of darkness may be overcome by the light of the world. Therefore, *no one for whom Christ performs his redemptive work can possibly be excluded from a theological investigation.* And for whom did Christ come? For unbelievers!

Therefore, a theology that lacks openness toward those without faith in Christ is a theology cut off from Christ's light. It is a theology devoid of charity toward the needy neighbor. It is also a theology that frustrates the redemption of men already Christian, for redemption is not complete for any individual until all the children of God now scattered abroad are gathered into one (John 11:52).

In order to fulfill this responsibility, there is no need for Christians to seek some common terrain with unbelievers by leaping out of their own skin and conde scendingly "adopting" for missionary purposes the unbelievers' viewpoint. For Christian existence itself is still mired in confusion and evil, though in Christ it is moving toward God's life and light. Without taking a single step Christians share in the darkness and despair and pride in which the unbeliever flounders. There can be no question of throwing him a lifepreserver from the safe elevation of serene faith. So far as a Christian wrestles with a real darkness, his theologizing will be open to the unbeliever. The fact that the believer seeks and moves toward the light does not mean that he has departed from the darkness. It means just the contrary. It means that he still knows the darkness, is still joined with unbelievers, though he also knows something more: he knows the Lord.

Therefore, if the theologian seeks the light of the Lord in relation to some darkness—the question of suffering, for example—he does so not to get away from his unbelieving brothers but to discover for himself and for them the light that dispels this darkness, so that his love for them may be complete. Though conducted wholly out of his own existence in relation to Christ, his reflection may open God's light to them and may thus liberate them from their enslavement to darkness, so that they may enter into the glory and openness that belong to the children of God.

IN SUMMARY

Let us summarize the four features of Christian theology that have just been sketched.

1. Theology is the work of men whose existence is oriented toward Jesus Christ, the life and the light of

God. As such it belongs to the church, the community of those who find themselves being redeemed by Christ.

2. Theology is the work of men who are in transition from darkness to light, from the darkness that Christ bears to the light that he brings. As such it belongs to the broken confessing church, the community of those who find themselves being condemned by Christ.

3. Theology is the work of men who meet Christ through the witness of the Bible, and as such it belongs to the church, the community of those who follow the testimony of the prophets and apostles.

4. Theology is the work of men who are called to serve their neighbors, as witnesses of Christ's redeeming work. As such it belongs to the evangelical church.

2

Demonism—The Spiritual Reality of Our Day

IN THE preceding chapter we identified a crucial problem of our time with which theology must be concerned. We also outlined the scope and nature of theological inquiry. Let us continue our investigation with a closer look at how violent suffering is actually experienced in our day.

Underlying all suffering is the fact that human beings are needy. They do not have the sources for their strength and life within themselves. They must be nourished, and nourished constantly. And this is true not only of their bodies but also of their minds. Their intellects crave the truth that comes from beyond them. Their wills crave something, anything that is desirable. Their imaginations hunger for a real beauty. In all ways their vitality—their identity as living persons—must be nourished.

This condition of need haunts every human being throughout his entire life, for he knows that there is some obscure and unaccountable discrepancy between what is available for him and what he requires for a rich life. Why isn't food better distributed? Why is television so boring? Why can he not accept his very limited abilities? Why can he not be satisfied in his marriage, or in his children? Why does his tooth have to begin aching just when there is an important committee meeting? Why, for all his concern and careful nurturing, did this friendship fall into disuse? These discrepancies between environment and need constitute suffering.

If men were not continually in need of nourishment and stimulation and distraction from the world, they could withdraw in various ways and so avoid the violence to which they are subjected. Religions that propose withdrawal as the way to escape suffering recognize that this way means the starvation and death of various human vitalities. And they believe that the goal of detachment is worth this price. But as long as men find their identities in the life which the world nourishes, they must open themselves to the world and thus leave themselves exposed to whatever abuses the world may inflict. For instance, if they involve themselves with other people, they may be violated by the greed or demands of their friends. The needs in human nature provide specific points of weakness which may be easily lacerated. But more important, this basic neediness requires men to adopt a posture of openness to the world, which in turn makes them ready victims of every convulsive power.

The Violence We Imagine

How do people today experience the sources of that violence which so grips and terrifies their imaginations? What is it that twists and torments men in their needy weakness?

Here, for instance, are the front-page stories in a paper at the end of a typical week: "State Department Warns China to Ease War Scare," "Tornadoes Spin Death and Destruction in Midwest," "Murderer Hanged as Barcelona Mob Storms Prison." On another typical day, we read: "Berserk Ex-soldier Shoots Doctor," "FBI Official Urges Sterner Treatment for Delinquents," "Plane Crashes with 17 Killed." This is the daily record, not perhaps of the world as it really is, but of those incidents which we consider newsworthy, of those events which are etched on our memories by headlines and photos.

A vast majority of these stories have something to do with violence—with a storm, or a murder, or a threat of war—with something that suddenly breaks into the lives of people bringing anguish or death. Violent disaster always has news value. But much more striking is the way in which the newspapers shape their stories of disaster by their style of presentation.

In the first place, they take great pains to emphasize, not what people do, but what they suffer, what is done to them. A man *is* murdered, a woman *is* raped, a house *is* blown over, an airplane *is* destroyed, a city *is* disturbed by riot, a country *is* under crisis. The newspaper reports constantly find the vividly human element in the suffering.

In the second place, newspapers tend to portray the cause of every disaster as something nonhuman, even though people are involved. Notice how, according to these stories, we are not troubled by particular boys but by "juvenile delinquency." Notice how the police are not battling specific men with individual problems, but are fighting a "crime wave." Words like "delinquency" and "wave" have the effect of making the agency acting in these incidents appear impersonal and inhuman. We do not know the murderer or the rapist. The airplane is forced down by a faceless government. The city is threatened by a faceless mob, the house destroyed by an invisible wind. And in the national crisis, even the most powerful leader seems, to some degree, a passive instrument of political forces which he cannot control or even understand.

Thirdly and most important, in these newspaper accounts there is the tendency to paint every disaster as if it were wholly *unexpected,* as if it broke into the normal routine of life from the unknown. In other words, there is something supernatural or transnatural about whatever is acting here. It does not even show traces of its coming beforehand. Several years ago there was a rash of incidents in which young children became tangled in plastic garment bags and suffocated. Here is the way *Time,* May 11, 1959, reported the news:

> In Manhattan, Nancy Alverson left her 2½-year-old daughter in their Greenwich Village apartment while she went shopping. Back in "a few minutes," she found the child dead of suffocation, with her head swathed in the adhering layers of a plastic garment bag.

Notice what pains were taken in this account to emphasize the normal routine of life, and therefore the completely unexpected and uncanny nature of the disaster. Mrs. Alverson was occupied with the everyday routine of shopping. It was a matter of only a few minutes, and nothing was involved but an ordinary garment bag. In the same fashion we are told how the murder victim was attacked while "on his usual walk," how the plane that crashed was "regularly scheduled," how the now-rioting city had been "perfectly calm" only a short while ago.

We should not imagine that this style of reporting is part of all journalism. In fact, one of the marks of our newspapers seventy-five years ago was their deliberate effort to *avoid the unexpected*. If there was a murder, we were first given a clear description of the locale, a brief history of the town, and some perfectly intelligible reasons for the deed. Similarly, if tension erupted in the Middle East, we read three columns of detailed history of the area before the crisis itself was described, and by then it seemed no crisis at all but the normal outworking of everything that had gone before. In those days, apparently, people wanted the newspapers to *remove* surprise from disaster, to take away any idea of accident, and to make every tragedy seem the obvious effect of previous events. Today the opposite is the case. Something is newsworthy only to the extent that it is unexpected. Even the international crisis is made to look like an accident. And the disorganized layout of the front page of the papers, the way unrelated items are bunched together, reinforces the impression that events fall into the human scene like an endless series of explosions.

Thus a picture begins to emerge from the newspapers in which men in the midst of life are suddenly crushed by an outbreak of violence from beyond the expected course of events. Call it "crime," call it "weather," call it "war," the picture is constantly the same.

Now the extraordinary thing is that if we turn from

the newspapers to the lives of ordinary people, we find everywhere a very similar picture. Consider, for example, the matter of a disease like cancer. At the top of their minds people know that cancer involves a mutation of organic cells, a natural phenomenon which will someday be prevented by natural remedies. But at a deeper, less self-conscious level they think of cancer primarily as the bearer of an energy of destruction. It is not so much a natural phenomenon as an instrument of obscure forces that it releases into the body. There is an occult quality associated in the public imagination with the power of cancer.

Do people today expect the resources of their bodies to take care of this danger? Not at all. No one today believes in his health as something powerful. Power—real decisive power—seems to belong to the disease. Even when men feel fine, glowing with juvenile vigor, they keep reminding themselves that it cannot last, that it is only momentary and may deceive them. Every day, therefore, they dutifully take their vitamins. Every month they dutifully pay their health insurance. And every year they dutifully submit to the medical examination, and wait for the X-ray to discover a spot somewhere on their lungs or for the smear to reveal cancer somewhere in their tissues.

This recent loss of confidence in health is connected with the recent way of picturing disease as a positive power. Eighty years ago, sickness was attributed to a lack or deficiency of health. A man became ill because of some weakening or impediment in the power of life that *naturally* belonged to his body. Consequently, if he was to be healed, it was not by putting power into him, but by making use of his own natural vitality, by activating it so that it would overcome whatever was wrong. Medicines did not cure him, but he cured himself by means of his body's own native resources.

It is just this way of seeing the body's vigor as the fundamental fact which is missing today. People do not tend to think of sickness primarily as weakening in *their* power of health, but as an invasion of some *outside* power into them. They experience disease as something that "attacks" them, or "grips" them, or "ravages" them —as if it were something real in its own right, a vital cancerlike force that lies hidden out in the world, waiting to strike. It is a reality that since childhood they have all been taught to picture in terms of germs or viruses— weird, indetectable terrors. And the obituaries and the fund drives are constantly reminding every man that for him this something may eventually be more powerful than all the health or all the science mankind can muster.

If the health of their own bodies is useless, how can people today help themselves? They fight fire with fire. Since they imagine themselves being victimized by strange powers, they try to marshal equally strange powers in their defense. They construct immense black machines studded with glittering eyes. They use invisible rays that penetrate everything. They invent uncanny drugs, with side effects no one can predict and names no one can pronounce, to be administered by long, sharp needles. In other words, against the obscure and occult forces of disease they have recourse to obscure counterforces. An occult quality hangs over the whole affair. And the hospital, the place where the battle is joined and where the monstrosities of medicine meet the monstrosities of disease, is a holy place of awe and stillness. Only the doctors and the nurses—the people specially initiated into the mysteries of this power struggle—can walk there with safety.

Yet even these defenses give no reassurance. What if physicians are able to conquer one disease? Remember that for Mrs. Alverson's baby, death came in an innocent garment bag. Suppose that you take all possible inoculations. Remember that even the air around us may be filled with deadly pollution. When Dr. Salk announced the success of his vaccine, was there a broad reassurance? Did anyone reduce his hospital insurance? For people today, health is not a permanent state. It is only that momentary condition when the powers of disease are held back and bide their time. Every day men wonder when they will attack. Several years ago Arthur Godfrey gave a representative statement when he waited to see if the tumor on his lung was cancerous. "I never felt better in my life," he said. "Then, boom, this horrible, skulking 'thing,' visible only as a ghostly shadow on an X-ray negative—this 'thing' that no longer gives me pain, probably because I cannot feel it through the cold, clutching fear that is gnawing at my vitals."

What appears in the sphere of health may also be found in other areas of contemporary experience. Consider, for instance, how people feel about the immediate world around them, about their homes and towns. Is this a good and fruitful place, where liberty thrives, where progress is on the move, and where order always has the last word against violence? On the contrary, people seem to have no confidence anymore in the powers of order.

They live in the midst of surging, dangerous machines, and that is how they experience their world.

We wake up in the morning to the hum of the heating unit. We eat breakfast by the hum of the refrigerator. We go to the office by the hum of the car. We talk to people through the hum of the telephone, and correspond by the hum of the dictaphone, and even think to the hum of the electric typewriter. We drink by the hum of the water cooler. We buy our food to the hum of the cash register. And finally, as the busy day ends in the quiet of the evening, we sit at home and dream to the hum of the television set. Everywhere we are enclosed by the strange forces that flow in these machines and that betray their terrific power only in this hardly audible noise. Beyond our homes and offices hums the city, a place of endless motion, which has no purpose and no rest, which pulsates twenty-four hours a day, 365 days a year. The city itself is a gigantic machine, throbbing with power and engulfing everyone in its own pointless haste. Even the suburbs, which were designed originally for escape from the city, have now been glutted with traffic and riddled with eight-lane superhighways.

In this world of humming power, everyone keeps on the watch. The heating unit works fine, but as the newspapers keep reminding us, it is quite capable of exploding and killing everyone in the house. The electric system is safe, provided the fuses are in order and the children do not play at the outlets. Gas stoves have to be checked at bedtime, just to be sure that the burners have been turned off. And when people leave their homes for the city they know that, for all their caution, they may happen to be in the way when the car lurches out of control, or when fire guts the theater, or when the juvenile gang attacks. They defend themselves as best they can—with safety fuses and safety valves, with air brakes and power brakes, with constant checkups by the repairman and comprehensive year-round insurance. Against the crime wave and other human explosions they maintain a police "force" with its squad cars and tear gas. Here, as in medicine, the defense must be comparable to the enemy. But when the plane is overdue, when the boy is out late with the car, when it is not certain whether they turned off the gas, people know that these defenses are useless.

In our day even romantic love—that first bastion of human self-indulgence—has become experienced as a potentially violent and destructive power. We are continually forced either to submit to it with violence or to suppress it into an empty habit. We are like Dr. Courrèges in Mauriac's novel *The Desert of Love*. We have a sterile homelife and a disturbed dream life. We have to keep choosing between the lie of decency, where we stifle the vigor and excitement of love, and the lie of gratification, where we degrade ourselves in unmanageable lust. In actual experience, love for adults is not the lush garden of the Orient filled with the gentle breezes and the quiet intoxication of fulfillment. Love, as Mauriac says, makes life into a burning desert. Every morning the newspaper tells of another person for whom love became frustration, became divorce, became murder. There is everywhere today the strong impression that sexual love, in its full potent reality, is a terribly destructive force. Man's only hope is to keep it calm, keep it weak, keep it habitual. As a character in Jean Anouilh's play *The Lark* suggests, vital love is not the business of honest people.

If we turn from the sphere of private life to the larger public world, we find that sufferings here also are attributed to the operation of *obscure destructive powers.* People still remember the good old days of economic optimism in America. Every man had his life in his own hands; the future was a golden road of opportunity; and millionaire success awaited anyone with get-up-and-go. But today no one really believes in our economy. Remembering 1929, they all know that a terrible momentum of disaster lurks within it, ready to break forth at any moment. They have their graphs and their charts to watch its every tremor. They tinker with the interest rate here and withdraw money from circulation there. Young people seek employment with a large concern which, they hope, will shelter them through all storms. But however steady the market, however promising the statistics, few ever seem to believe in our prosperity. The anxious worrying about the economy goes on and on and on, at the dinner table, at the university, at the White House, like an endless conference of baffled doctors around a sick bed. For us, prosperity is no more the foundation of life than is health. It is merely that temporary condition between the two monsters of destruction, inflation on the one hand and depression on the other.

There is finally the international scene. Not long ago, life between nations was thought of in terms of the vigor and success of human civilization. In every out-of-the-way corner of the world new territories opened to man's creative touch. For the first time, the hidden resources of these places began to contribute to the betterment of human life, and primitive peoples began to taste civilization. Of course, wars occurred when the positive dynamic of one nation interfered with that of another. But there was nothing dreadful here. War was accepted as a natural instrument of national policy, painful to be sure, but given the realities of a situation, it often seemed like a reasonable and expedient thing to do. It was conducted by men, controlled by men, and pursued for the sake of genuinely human values.

Today such a viewpoint seems incredibly remote. The international scene is now dominated by one thing alone: the threat of total war. This is not war in the old sense, a means for the advancement of human goals, where certain advantages of national life are at stake. This is war in the new sense, the pure power of annihilation, which yields nothing but destruction and which therefore stands wholly outside the bounds of rational purpose. Today we do not think of war as a human activity, and anyone who deliberately undertakes it, like Hitler, must be mad. He must have lost his human ways and fallen under the control of the ferocity which he unleashes.

Nevertheless, though men think of war as an utterly inhuman event, opposed by all true humanity, at the same time they have no confidence at all that mankind can get rid of its threat. Their only hope is to keep it at a distance, and to do so by means of huge defenses, incredible weapons, and an emphatic policy of retaliation. In other words, on the international scene people have no confidence in rational persuasion or signed treaties or any of the other *human* devices used by our forefathers. The best that they can do is to shelter themselves against war behind the power of war itself. They cannot imagine any defense but the threat of total war. Peace depends on being able to unleash war. Just as they experience bodily health and economic prosperity, they think of peace also as a cold war, a ceaseless fight against destructive powers.

This long review of modern fears is not meant to deny that men ever enjoy their securities. Of course, they know the vigor of healthy bodies, the affection of parents and children, the assurance of a relatively steady income and a relatively peaceful town. What must be emphasized is the peculiar preoccupations of men today, as if the only powers that count are *essentially destructive,* and as if these powers are lurking constantly just beyond their range of vision, waiting to break in upon them.

The belief that in the end these powers will always have the last word gives our age a certain grim wisdom. It can understand Camus, when in his novel *The Plague* he criticizes the townspeople of Oran for not taking seriously the terrible epidemic that has struck them:

Our townsfolk were like everybody else, wrapped up in themselves; in other words they were humanists: they disbelieved in pestilences. A pestilence isn't a thing made to man's measure; therefore we tell ourselves that pestilence is a mere bogy of the mind, a bad dream that will pass away. But it doesn't always pass away and, from one bad dream to another, it is men who pass away. . . . Our townsfolk were not more to blame than others; they forgot to be modest, that was all, and thought that everything still was possible for them; which presupposed that pestilences were impossible. They went on doing business, arranged for journeys, and formed views. How should they have given a thought to anything like plague, which rules out any future, cancels journeys, silences the exchange of views. They fancied themselves free, and no one will ever be free so long as there are pestilences.

Using Camus' terms, we can say that the people in America today are not humanists. They do not fancy themselves free. They know that there are pestilences. As the newspapers teach them day after day, life seems to be in the hands of unseen forces which are ever ready to attack them—to shatter the security of their bodies, or the security of their loves, or the security of their land. And worst of all, they know that disaster may strike just when the situation seems most secure, just when, like Arthur Godfrey, they "never felt better" in their lives, just when, like Mrs. Alverson, they were shopping, just at the height of prosperity in 1929, or just after the perfect agreement had been reached at Munich.

THE NEW SHAPE OF THE DEMONIC

From this brief survey of the modern way of imagining violence, we may draw two conclusions. First of all, people today apparently find the most decisive manifestation of power in that which *destroys,* rather than in that which produces or preserves. In other words, we are in a situation today in which the attitude of *dread* has come to dominate over all others.

Secondly, we must say that as concretely experienced, these destructive powers have a very peculiar character: they intrude upon the human scene and then withdraw with such arbitrary suddenness that they cannot be rationally identified. They have no faces of their own, no names. They simply erupt. And there is no effort to place them when they are absent. Where does the power that breeds war exist in time of peace? Where now is the energy of inflation and depression that constantly threatens our economy? Nowhere and everywhere.

Once we identify these two features in the modern experience of violence, we can recognize it as a fairly common and worldwide phenomenon in the history of human religion. Technically, it might be called the experience of the *demonic*.

We must not think of demons as little humanlike figures with horns and pitchforks. Demons are not specific *things* at all, and are certainly not human. They represent, rather, that peculiar energy of destruction which is met in an infected wound, say, or in a conflict between brothers. The demonic is not the wound itself, but that power, present in the wound, which generates the infection and eventually devours the entire life of the body. In a misunderstanding between brothers, the demonic appears, not in the hostility itself, which is a perfectly human feeling, but in the dynamic of hate that magnifies the hostility into inhuman proportions, until it becomes an insatiable rage.

By its very character, therefore, the demonic has no shape or form of its own. Its essence is to twist and break apart the forms of other things, to stunt human growth, to disrupt the social order, to misshape animals and trees, to obstruct the fruitfulness of the earth. The demonic is only known by virtue of the destruction that it causes. Therefore, when men try to represent it in pictures, they often present it as the twisted form of some vital natural creature—a fire-breathing dragon, a bloated snake, a sadistic human figure with goatlike features.

Ever since the sixteen hundreds and the advent of natural science, Western civilization has dispensed with the need for such an idea as the demonic. In 1642 René Descartes, the French philosopher, proposed that all reality under God consisted of mind and matter. Mind represented the human sphere and everything nonhuman was embraced under "matter." According to Descartes, matter was a realm of rational order, open to scientific inquiry and accessible to empirical observation.

The significance of this reasonable proposal is easy to see. If true, it means that there can be no occult powers or mysteriously demonic forces out there in the world. Whatever is not human is, by definition or by axiom, objectively observable and scientifically understandable "matter." Enlightened skeptics then looked upon devils as the superstitious invention of primitive fear, while conservative Christians converted them into quasi-human minds that lacked bodies and went about doing evil. In any case, no one had any idea of the demonic, that is, of occult powers that suddenly intrude upon the human scene bringing destruction. There was considerable optimism, in fact, about the nonhuman realm, and only the human realm, with its sin and tyranny and injustice, posed the serious problems. The Christian church was caught up in these new attitudes as much as was every other group.

It can be said that what has happened in American life today is the rediscovery of the demonic. People seem to see the world as filled with shapeless ferocities that come and go. What terrifies them about cancer is not any particular virus or organic structure that may cause it, but the insidious vitality of death which it releases in the body. They focus their experience of war, not upon the good that may result, but upon the terrific violence that it unleashes into the world. And like the demons of other ages, war is believed to take possession of the human mind as well as to disrupt the environment. Its energy can not only overthrow institutions and demolish cities, but can even invade a man's inner life and carry him to inconceivable excesses of brutality—the concentration camps, Coventry, Dresden. The fact that this experience of the demonic is not yet very self-conscious does not minimize its importance.

It is now possible to understand more clearly why, to our age, violence represents evil in its most naked and horrible form. People today see in such violence the operation of forces that are peculiarly and essentially destructive, and that no properly human kind of power is able to withstand. But once events of violence are experienced in this way, then the whole question of God comes into view. If our world is subject to these terribly destructive forces, how can the good God of Christianity be said to be Lord of this world? What confidence can we have in him if he is not able—or not willing—to obstruct these demonic forces? In other words, because people today feel the impact of evil chiefly in terms of *abusive power,* they are asking about God chiefly in terms of his *redemptive power.* And in the churches they hear very little on this theme.

THE DEMONIC AS THE DECISIVE FORM OF EVIL

In the New Testament portrayal of Jesus, he is shown to be everywhere engaged with what must be called *energies of violation*. His whole work of redemption, in fact, is explicitly related precisely to that demonic form of evil and to that violent form of suffering which preoccupies people today.

Everyone is familiar with the New Testament account of disease and insanity as demon possession. What is less clearly recognized is that even the evil of human sin is understood, not as a perversity that originates in man, but as man's entanglement with and subjection to demonic forces. For instance, those who perform the supreme sin, in that they seek to kill Jesus, are said to be of the devil their father, who was a murderer from the beginning and had no truth in him (John 8:44). Man's sin is presented not primarily as his perverse will or corrupt nature, but rather, as his enslavement to a diabolic kingdom. Along these same lines the New Testament always sees human evil as consummating in acts of violence and supremely, of course, in the act of murder. King Herod, for example, has John the Baptist slaughtered in a grotesque parody of keeping one's promise. (Mark 6:22-26.) The Pharisees' perversity with the law is indicated by the fact that they do *violence* to the people. They prohibit their being healed on the Sabbath (Mark 3:3-5), and they "bind heavy burdens upon them which are hard to bear" (Matt. 23:4).

Rudolf Bultmann would have us see through and beyond this notion of the demonic in the New Testament. It is a mythological element and should be removed, he says, "because it is different from the conception of the world which has been formed and developed by science . . . and which has been accepted by all modern men" (*Jesus Christ and Mythology*). Bultmann is here speaking as a member of what is now the older generation. He expresses the viewpoint of those who were educated at a time when science seemed immediately and evidently to provide the truth about the world, and who firmly believed in the Descartes' principle that everything non-human in the world is constituted by matter.

Of course, it is not necessary for Christians in all ages and circumstances to contrive some idea of the demonic simply in order to imitate the content of the New Testament superficially. At the same time, it is also not necessary for Christians to be bound to the Cartesian mentality which developed in the seventeenth century and to deny the presence of anything occult or demonic in the world. The church is not bound to make human sin the last and most serious form of evil, or to see Christ's redemptive work simply as the forgiveness and removal of sin. In fact, since there is everywhere today what Camus calls a sense of pestilences and a hypnotic dread of violent suffering, any effort to restrict evil and redemption within the purely human sphere can only seem like a pathetic evasion of genuine evil. The demonic has replaced sin as the decisive form of evil, and therefore as the decisive arena for Christ's victory—or impotence.

Our next step will be to inquire about the kind of powerfulness that is operative in Jesus and that liberates men from the powers of violence.

3

Service as the Power of God

IN ALL his teaching and deeds Jesus stands forth as the advocate of love. It is important to recognize, however, that the love that concerns him has a particular character: it is essentially an activity of *self-expenditure* for another's need.

We have a striking portrayal of this in his parable of the good Samaritan. (Luke 10: 30-37.) For to what goodness in the Samaritan's behavior does Jesus carefully draw our attention? One normally thinks that the primary good here must be the *effects* of the Samaritan's charity on the wounded man—the way in which he helped the latter to escape death, to find relief for his pain, and eventually to recover his health. Curiously enough, however, this aspect of the situation does not stand out at all. In fact, Jesus *never once* mentions the consequences of this service for the wounded man— whether his wounds were healed, whether he lost an eye, whether the Samaritan's charity produced a spiritual change in him, calling him, perhaps, to take a new and kindlier interest in people.

What Jesus does emphasize in his narrative is not the

results of the Samaritan's action but his *way of acting* with unlimited and single-minded self-giving. For instance, Jesus does not say that the Samaritan simply bound up the man's wounds, but that he poured on them oil and wine. In describing the journey to the inn, Jesus notes that this required the Samaritan to walk, since the latter apparently had only a single animal on which the wounded man had to be set. At the inn Jesus stresses how the Samaritan did not then go about his own business, but spent all night taking care of the man.

Jesus climaxes this portrayal with the most astonishing point of all. When in the morning the Samaritan came to settle the bill, he did not pay for just the expenses to date. He agreed to bear the full cost of any future expense that might be required for the wounded man. "Take care of him," Jesus has him say to the innkeeper, "and whatever more you spend, I will repay you when I come back." Jesus thus makes his point perfectly clear: what is good about the Samaritan is the unqualified liberality with which he expends himself for the other's needs.

This kind of love is the constant theme of Jesus' teachings. "What shall I do to inherit eternal life?" asks a man who had fulfilled all the commandments. "Go," Jesus replies, "and sell all that you have to feed the poor." (Mark, ch. 10.) In another context he declares:

"If a man wants to sue you for your shirt, let him have your coat as well. If a man in authority makes you go one mile, go with him two. Give when you are asked to give; and do not turn your back on a man who wants to borrow." (Matt. 5: 40-42, NEB.)

Jesus does not identify love primarily with producing good in the lives of others. Nor does he equate it with what we call "philanthropy," that is, the giving of *surplus* wealth or *surplus* time to help others. On the contrary a man only begins to love as Jesus commands when he gives out of what is essential to him, out of what he cannot "afford." For Jesus, it is the deliberate and uninhibited willingness to expend *oneself* for another that constitutes love. And Jesus' own existence is the most overwhelming demonstration of this way. From first to last he lived a life of self-expending service, walking the second mile, giving everything to feed the poor, and even laying down his life for his friends.

A SHOCKINGLY IMPRACTICAL CREED

In this parable of the good Samaritan we come face-to-face with the shocking impracticality of Jesus' teaching, an impracticality that no amount of "helpful" interpretation can remove. If a man really possesses a readiness to expend himself for others, will they not take advantage of him? Will they not soon take all his clothes and borrow all his money? Of course, says Jesus. Of course, if you live in this way, you will be used up by others. Of course, they will take everything you have. That is why you should expect this self-expenditure to lead sooner or later to your death. He is quite clear and unafraid about the practical implications of his teaching. But this, he says, is exactly what you *want* people to do. It is the essence of your love to want to be expended for others, and even to die for others. "There is no greater love than this," he says, "that a man should lay down his life for his friends." (John 15: 13, NEB.)

Therefore, when Jesus identifies love with self-expenditure, he means just that, the real expending and spilling out of the self. There are no magical tricks here, no secret doors to escape from the real self-emptying involved. There is no suggestion that, while men may *appear* to walk the extra mile, or appear to sell all that they have for the poor, or appear to die for their friends, they are all the time accumulating riches for themselves. There is no suggestion that the expression of such love will bring some pleasure to the giver or serve to build up a good reputation with God. "If any man would come after me," Jesus says, "let him deny himself." (Luke 9: 23.) Self-denial is inseparable from such love.

There is also no secret expectation that other people will be so irresistibly impressed by such kindness that they will suddenly become kind themselves. On the contrary, Jesus is quite emphatic that, far from impressing or converting people, this way may only make them contemptuous, may even encourage their worst tendencies to victimize and exploit.

But how can Jesus propose such a creed as a way for the enhancement of human life? He himself gives us a perfectly clear answer. He is not afraid that his kind of loving involves the death of life as we usually think of it, because for him this loving is *itself the fullness of true life*. By his advocacy of love, then, Jesus does not mean to give people a new and superior means for achieving such life as they have always sought. He means to redefine the very character of life.

Once Jesus' message is seen in these terms, we are able to understand why he sees no reason that the act of giving to others and even of dying for others should involve any secret reward. Because such giving and such dying are themselves life at its richest, no rewards are needed. Without the addition of a single benefit or the consideration of a single consequence, such activity in and by itself constitutes the fullness of man's power and vitality and effectiveness and joy. When does a grain of wheat become fruitful? Jesus asks. Not when it is living on the stalk, but when it falls to the earth and dies. (John 12: 24.) Being dynamically alive does not consist in heaping up treasures or achievements or reputations for oneself. It consists in expending oneself for others.

The word "self-expenditure" may therefore be misleading. It may suggest that expending oneself for others is a real loss and deprivation of one's life. On the contrary, it is the enhancement of one's life. Self-expenditure is self-fulfillment. He who loses his life is *thereby* finding it. Loving is *itself* life, and not just a means to life. He who expends himself for his neighbor, even to death, truly lives. But he who lives for himself and avoids death truly dies. "He who does not love remains in death." (I John 3: 14.)

Regardless of the wisdom of the world or the testimony of experience, Jesus seems to be saying: I myself am the measure and criterion for the fullness of human existence. And since life in me takes the form of unlimited self-expenditure—of walking the second mile, of giving everything to feed the poor, of laying down my life for my friends—then that is the form of true life and joy for every man. "I," he says, "am the way, and the truth, and the life; no one comes to the Father, but by me." (John 14: 6.) "This is my commandment, that you love one another *as I have loved you*." (Ch.

15: 12.) And in a passage from The First Letter of John, the writer makes perfectly clear how Jesus has loved us: "By this we know love, that he laid down his life for us; and we ought to lay down our lives for the brethren" (ch. 3: 16).

In other words, when a man lives as Jesus did, and spills out his life for others, either in one decisive moment or gradually over a whole lifetime of daily attrition and impoverishment, then he is truly alive. If he lives to expand himself rather than to expend himself, he is empty and dead. His doing has no power and bears no fruit. His apparent vitality is really sterile. His sitting impressively at the head of the table and being served by relatives, hairdressers, newsboys, and press agents is an impotent masquerade. His seeming powerfulness is like the house that a man builds upon the sand: it has no real strength and topples before the wind (Matt. 7:27).

Why should all this be so? Granted that Jesus lived a life of service and called others to do the same, why identify the fullness of human being with his very peculiar behavior? After all, quite other styles of life have been advocated. Some have found fulfillment in the life of thought. Karl Marx was enthusiastic about a collective existence. The ancient Stoics saw the importance of being disengaged from the world. The modern existentialists champion a life of radical decision. And none of these ways, at least, call upon men to expend themselves for others even to the point of death. None of these require men to reverse their usual understanding of what constitutes life and what constitutes death. Why should there be confidence that Jesus' way is the real key to human fulfillment?

This brings us to the second level in the teaching of the New Testament. The power and life present in Jesus are not simply aspects of his human being, but belong to God. Jesus is the presence of God himself in the human scene. "In him," Paul writes, "the fulness of God was pleased to dwell." (Col. 1: 19.) Jesus' self-expending, therefore, was not a form that he put on himself to see how well it would work. It was not a technique that he was testing to see how nicely it would help him to manage his career or improve his relations with people and with God. He did not stand in the carpenter shop at Nazareth, surveying various human possibilities and perhaps consulting the local library, until he came to the decision to adopt service as his style. He was what he was solely because of what God is, for he was the presence of God in the midst of men. His walking the second mile, his giving all that he had to feed the poor, his laying down his life for his friends, were not merely human actions but the actions of divinity itself.

Therefore, in his self-expenditure what is being exhibited is not just the power native to human life but the power of God himself, so far as men share in it. In other words, Jesus is not telling men how to reshape their lives. He is telling them what their lives become when they participate in God's own life, in what the New Testament calls "eternal life." What their lives become is a momentum of self-expending service. Such service, therefore, should be thought of not simply as the improvement of human existence but as its transfiguration and exaltation, for it is God who is self-expending love. It is *God's* own love that stands forth in and as Jesus Christ and that informs the loving self-expenditure of men for one another. God's love, John writes, "was disclosed to us in this, that he sent his only Son into the world to bring us life. . . . *God himself* dwells in us if we love one another; *his* love is brought to perfection within us" (I John 4:9, 12, NEB).

Christian faith looks upon Jesus as the power of the one and only God from whom all other powers in heaven and earth derive their real powerfulness. If Jesus discloses the unopposable power of love, it can only be because this love is the power of God himself.

The startling aspect of this faith becomes clear, however, only when we reverse the order of this sentence, and say, not that Jesus represents the power of love, but that the power of God reveals itself in and *as* Jesus. In that man's concrete, empirical existence, which is to say, in those acts of, and commands for, loving self-expenditure which are recorded in the four Gospels, we have exhibited the power by which God rules the world. Jesus is not seen as the revelation of God to us in his heavenly condition as the eternal Son, or in his resurrected condition as the glorified Christ, or in his coming on clouds of glory at the end of the ages, for we are not presented with him concretely in any of these conditions. He is the revelation of God precisely in his serving, in his humbling himself in obedience even unto death (Phil. 2:8).

We spoke above of how Jesus follows a *kind of life* that contradicts all our assumptions about life because it seems to involve death. Jesus exhibits a powerfulness that contradicts all our assumptions about power, because in normal terms he seems to be utterly weak. He does not vindicate himself with the *kind of powerfulness* that we have always admired. He does not assert himself, preserve himself, or impose his will upon others. Obviously, then, the God revealed in Jesus Christ is not just any God, or even a being who is endowed with all sorts of supreme attributes. This God is very peculiar, and in a fundamental way very ungodlike.

THE POWER THAT IS WEAKNESS

In his teachings and in his life Jesus stands completely opposed to all powers that victimize, to all the energies of violence that rage through this world. He allows no ground for treating these forces as really good, to be affirmed as agents of God's will and expressions of God's power and, therefore, to be allowed to run their course. He sets himself against all those persons and realities which use their power to cause suffering.

The reason for this comes out very clearly in a passage in the Gospel of Luke. There the disciples argue with each other about which of them is the greatest.

"And ... [Jesus] said to them, 'The kings of the Gentiles exercise lordship over them; and those in authority over them are called benefactors. But not so with you; rather let the greatest among you become as the youngest, and the leader as one who serves. For which is the greater, one who sits at table, or one who serves? Is it not the one who sits at table? But I am among you as one who serves.'" (Ch. 22: 25-27.)

In this passage Jesus sets himself in contrast to the Gentile lords in terms of his relation to *human weakness and need*. For the Gentile world, neediness is precisely the condition in which a man may be violated by a superior power, and a lord is one who can exercise such power. The Gentile lords stand in authority and demand submission because of their capacity to exercise violent power. Of course, they may not choose to execute this capacity. They may give richly to their subjects. Nevertheless, this is what undergirds their authority, their "greatness."

Jesus makes clear that the divine power in him vindicates its powerfulness in the face of human need in just the opposite way. It does not dominate, threaten, or impose violence; it *serves*. In this connection it is no accident that Jesus undertakes his mission to the poor and not to the rich, to the sinful and not to the righteous, to the weak and not to the strong, to the dying and not to those full of life. For with these vessels of need God most decisively vindicates *his* peculiar kind of power, his power of service whereby the poor are fed, the sinful are forgiven, the weak are strengthened, and the dying are made alive.

Therefore, in the perspective of the New Testament, what is involved in the problem of violent suffering is no incidental matter, but touches the very nature of divine power. Jesus sets himself in total opposition to all modes of violence and to every kind of powerfulness that must establish itself in the Gentile way, that is, by being able to do violence to the weak and needy. Such so-called power is not an aspect of, but rather the very opposite of, God's power. And therefore, since God alone is the author and ground of all real power, this energy of violence is not actually powerful at all. Its power is only pretension.

At the heart of the Christian faith in Jesus is the knowledge that true power belongs only to God. The distinctive mark of God's power is service and self-giving. And in this world such power belongs only to him who serves. In the light of such a faith, the Christian has no final fear before the pretentious claims of violent power.

If there is a Christian solution to the problem of suffering, therefore, it lies in such an understanding of the power of God.

4

Self-giving as the Inner Life of God

WE HAVE been speaking of God with respect to the power that he exercises toward men. But we must go farther and ask: *What is God within himself, in his inner nature and fundamental character?*

In the Christian world today almost no one talks about God himself. Christians are preoccupied instead either with God's acts—with the good things that he gives us and the moral demands that he makes on us, with Jesus whom he sent and the church that he created—or with the human response to God's acts—with *our* faith and *our* doubt, with *our* believing and unbelieving. But attention never seems to pass beyond these events on the human scene to God as he is in himself. Even a text like "God is love" is taken to refer, not to God in himself, but to what his actions do on our behalf.

In fact, as will become clear in the next chapter, there is a great danger in this modern procedure. If God's acts of service and love toward men are not grounded upon the nature and life that God has within himself, they may seem arbitrary and unreliable.

It was to avoid this danger that the fathers in the early

church made a distinction between two kinds of Christian knowledge. There is, first, the kind of knowledge with which we are familiar today, the knowledge of God's acts and of the results of his acts. The early fathers called this knowledge "economy," from the Greek word for "work." Economy was the knowledge of God's works, and that meant not only knowledge of his two great works, creating the world and saving men, but also every detail in the life of the world that might have to do with God. Matters of life and death, good and evil, order and disorder, the governing of the state and the significance of the home, all belonged to economy.

Alongside of economy, however, the fathers insisted that the Christian also had a knowledge of God himself, and this knowledge they called "theology." It was not gained by looking at God directly. In this life, men never see God. They only see his works. But in and through his works they come to know him as he is in himself. God is light. He is unobstructed openness. When we meet him in his actions, therefore, we meet him in his full openness toward us. In fact, the fathers believed that the works that God does toward us are done not for their own sakes but primarily to enable us to know him. As it is said in the Gospel of John, "This is eternal life, that they know thee the only true God, and Jesus Christ whom thou hast sent" (ch. 17: 3). In every theological investigation, it is important to pass on from "economy," the knowledge of what God does in Christ, to "theology," the knowledge of what or who God is.

If theology is concerned with the knowledge of who or what God is, then one may say that the content of theology is the *doctrine of the Trinity*. For the doctrine of the Trinity is just this: an attempt to clarify the nature of God who reveals himself in Jesus Christ.

Is the Trinity an Outmoded Doctrine?

In the last two centuries the doctrine of the Trinity has been almost a dead letter for much Christian thought. Schleiermacher thought it in need of revision, and even so orthodox a figure as Karl Barth gives it a routine treatment in the first volume of his *Church Dogmatics*. At the popular level it is considered to be nothing but a feat of intellectual nonsense. God is supposed to be one and three at the same time. If you find this unintelligible, that simply proves how incomprehensible is the reality of God and how bold is the Christian faith! Needless to say, any doctrine that makes God into a numerical monstrosity and that treats his presence in Christ as serving to stupefy the human mind should be rejected out of hand.

There is a further difficulty. The Trinity did not become a central focus for Christian reflection until the fourth century. This troubles those who have a static view of Christian truth and who believe that such truth can only be what stands forth as self-evident in the New Testament. But such a fixed notion of truth has not prevailed throughout the history of the Christian church. On the contrary, each age penetrates and focuses on the good news in its own way, and if first-century Christians were gripped by the resurrection, nineteenth-century Christians centered on service to the neighbor. There is a depth and manifoldness about the revelation of God in Jesus, and the theological preoccupations of no single period in the church's history should be allowed to tyrannize the whole church.

The Trinity was clearly *the* concern of Eastern Christians of the fourth century. What we must ask is not, Was this concern also central for the New Testament writers? but rather, Is this rooted in the Biblical presentation of Jesus? Is this doctrine truly offered as a clarification and penetration of the powerfulness of God which gathers men into itself through Jesus? I hope that my exposition of the doctrine will show that the answer to both of these questions is yes.

THE UNFINISHED WORK OF NICAEA

By far the best way to approach the question of the Trinity is to examine the struggles that went on between Athanasius, the bishop of Alexandria in Egypt, and Arius, a priest in the church of Alexandria. This conflict grew out of the Council of bishops held at Nicaea near Constantinople in A.D. 325.

The creed adopted by the majority of bishops at that Council states the decisive point: Jesus Christ is "the Son of God, begotten of the Father, Only-begotten, that is, from the substance of the Father, God from God, Light from Light, Very God from Very God, begotten not made, one in substance with the Father."

Two points stand out here. First, there is the insistence that the divine power met in Jesus—what is called the "Son" of God—is generated from God the Father. After the analogy of human generation, the Son derives his reality from the very being of the Father. He is not made by God from some reality external to God; he is not created out of nothing, like the Creation. He is begotten from the very "substance" of God.

Secondly, and following from this first point, the creed asserts that through this process of begetting, the Son receives the *full measure* of God's reality. He himself is fully and genuinely divine, "God from God, Light from Light, Very God from Very God." Here the bishops at Nicaea were simply repeating a theme found so prominently in the New Testament, especially in the Gospel of John. There we read that the Father has given all things to the Son, all his knowledge, all his power, all his glory (chs. 16: 15; 3: 35). The New Testament speaks of the Son, whom men encounter in Jesus Christ, as the perfect image of God the Father (Heb. 1: 3) and as having complete equality with God the Father (Phil. 2: 6).

There is a third point about the Son, which is not explicit in the Creed of Nicaea, but which became very important in the later discussion. The Son in his own reality does everything for the sake of the Father. This again is simply the development of a theme in the Gospel of John, where it is said that the Son never seeks to do his own will (ch. 5: 30), never acts on his own authority (ch. 8: 28), never offers his own teaching (ch. 7: 16). In short, the Son never seeks his own glory but only the glory of the Father who sent him (v. 18). If the Son receives the fullness of divine glory from the Father, he offers all that he has received back to the Father. Therefore, whoever believes in the Son or praises the Son or adores the glory of the Son does not really believe in or praise or adore the Son as such, but actually believes in and praises and adores the Father. For everything believable or praiseworthy or adorable which the Son possesses in himself he offers to the glory of the Father.

Here, in summary, are the three elements in the Nicene position: the Son that men encounter in Jesus and as Jesus (1) is derived from the very being of the Father, (2) is completely equal to the Father in all respects (i.e., he receives all that the Father has), and (3) fully glorifies the Father, offering as praise to the Father all that he has received.

Such was the Nicene position, accepted by the majority at the Council. But in the years that followed, Athanasius took a step beyond this and thereby raised an important issue. The Nicene Creed clearly asserts that the Son is derived from God the Father, is fully equal to God the Father, and lives for the glory of God the Father. But the creed does not make clear to what extent the Son's generation from God, equality with God, and praise of God are an *essential and permanent dimension within God's eternal being*. Might it be that God is fully and completely God in his mode as the Father? However divine the Son may be, might the Father's generation of the Son still constitute an action of God over and above what he is in his basic divine reality? Might the Son, for all his likeness to the Father, still be accidental to God's being as God? The creed insists on the full divinity of the Son, but it does not insist on the eternal and essential place of Sonship within divinity. And that was the theme that Athanasius developed. Generation, he maintained, belongs to the permanent, eternal being of God. This is an aspect—no, this is *the* essential aspect—of God's divinity.

Does God Need a Son?

The best way to appreciate what this step by Athanasius involved is to review the attacks that his opponent Arius leveled against it. Arius defended the position that what men encounter in Jesus, as the Son of God, is not the fullness of God himself, but only *a creature,* though in fact he is the first creature, through whom all others are made. Furthermore, according to Arius, to confuse the power in Jesus with God himself is a blasphemy of the highest kind. For what is at stake, he contends, is the very nature of God's divinity.

Arius was convinced that divinity—genuine full divinity—*cannot be communicated.* It cannot be passed from one being to another; it cannot be generated or begotten or produced. For divinity, he says, by its very nature, is *wholly self-contained,* is fully *complete in itself.* It has no need for change, no need to extend itself or communicate itself or generate itself. Wholly by itself and within itself it is completely *absolute.* "We know," he writes, "there is one God, alone unbegotten, alone eternal, alone without beginning, alone true, alone immortal . . ."

On the basis of this exalted notion of God's divinity, Arius is appalled at the Nicene idea of God's begetting a Son from his inner substance. First, he says, this shatters God's unity and introduces into the divine being an element of plurality, process, and change.

Secondly, to impute to God multiplicity and process is actually to think of him in material terms. For immaterial entities cannot be counted like physical objects, and cannot generate their like in the manner of animals.

Thirdly, Arius argued that anything which derives its reality from beyond itself is excluded by that very fact from being divine. *Divinity in its very essence is underived and self-sufficient.* If the power met in Jesus is called "Son of God" by the New Testament writers, Arius observed, that is simply their way of saying that this power is dependent on God, constituted by God, and is therefore *not itself God.*

Fourthly, to apply the notion of "begetting" to God's own substance is to take a notion from Greek mythology and to apply it illegitimately to the Biblical God. According to the entire Hebrew tradition, and therefore also according to the New Testament, the model for understanding God in his activity is not the model of generation and sexual reproduction, so dear to Greek mythology, but the model of the artisan who makes and the king who governs. The Arian party therefore looked upon this theological use of the model of begetting by Athanasius and his supporters as one of the most corrupt paganizations of Christianity.

Fifthly, Arius was convinced that self-contained absoluteness should characterize God just as much in his dealings with creatures as in his own nature. That means that in his rule over the world, while things are completely determined by him, *he himself must not be directly involved with them.* That is to say, he must exercise his rule only *through an agent,* never becoming directly active himself. That agent, Arius insisted, is the Son. In his view, then, for Athanasius to treat the derived powerfulness in Jesus as fully God not only violates God's character of being wholly underived and self-contained, but also drags God down to the give-and-take of direct action with the world. But God is too absolute to touch the world directly. His first creature, made flesh in Jesus, is the agent through whom he carries out all his dealings with creation.

Such was the Arian position. God is divine because he does not have the deficient, inadequate kind of reality that belongs to creatures. He is not divided, he is not dependent on another, he is not derived from another.

Indeed, according to Arius, if God were to give his being to another, were to beget another from himself, and if his reality were capable of being received by another, then such reality would immediately cease to be the reality of God. It would be just another of those divisible, changeable, derivable, dependent kinds of existence which we have around us all the time. It would lack the peculiar glory and absoluteness of God, and would therefore cease to merit our *human worship*. If God is truly God, then Jesus as the Son of God is derived from God and dependent on God, and therefore cannot himself be God. He must be a creature. "The Son," Arius states, "is not equal to God in any way, but is made out of nothing by God. The Father, who is alone without cause and without beginning and who therefore is alone God, is completely alien to the Son in essence."

In all the history of Christianity there has hardly been so sophisticated, so Biblically grounded, and so thoroughgoing a theology of God's transcendence as that developed by Arius and his followers. Their whole concern was to honor God by setting him above and in contrast to his creatures. They sought to preserve the glory of God by divesting his reality of all those weaknesses and deficiencies which mark his creatures, and by giving him the most absolute kind of mastery over his creatures.

When in the face of this Arian theology, Athanasius boldly insisted that the Son is completely derived from the Father, *and* is completely equal to the Father and an eternal permanent dimension of God's reality, he was repudiating the Arian notion of God. He was saying that the unique power met in Jesus, which the New Testament calls the "Son of God," is a derived powerfulness, a produced powerfulness, and therefore a dependent powerfulness, and in that special sense, a *needy powerfulness*. Yet Athanasius also insisted that having this derived, dependent, and needy form of power does not in the least compromise the Son's full and unqualified divinity. He is not one iota less fully divine because he is generated and produced.

In other words, the fact that the Father is completely uncaused and the Son is completely caused does not have any bearing on the status of their divinity. Though derived and dependent, though constantly given all his reality from beyond himself, the Son is nevertheless still entirely equal to the Father.

Therefore, according to Athanasius, Arius is wrong from the ground up. He is wrong in terms of his doctrine of God, and he is wrong in terms of the property of God which he thinks should arouse man's religious reverence. Being absolute, being self-contained, being superior and transcendent—in short, being like the Gentile lords in Jesus' saying—is not the essential mark of divinity. Furthermore, to worship God because he is absolute, to admire God because he is wholly self-contained, to bow down to God because he is superior and transcendent over his creatures, and immune from all need and lacking all dependence—is to worship him falsely. In fact, it is not to worship the true God at all, but some false God. For the true God exists eternally—in one of his modes—as the Son, that is, in the state of dependence.

The true God, therefore, will always disappoint that Arian feeling of reverence for the absolute which lies in the heart of every man.

A Relationship of Total Self-giving

Now we are in a position to see the real problem in the doctrine of the Trinity. The problem is not, How can the three persons of the Trinity, each genuinely distinct from the others, and each fully God, be conceived as one God who is utterly single and completely indivisible? This is a secondary and somewhat specious problem that arises only for those who feel obligated to reduce their religious understanding to a system of consistent propositions. Athanasius does not dwell on this problem. And all the historians of Christian doctrine—all those who imagine that this reconciling of threeness and oneness was the great problem facing the defenders of the Nicene Creed—have failed to understand Arius.

Again, the problem is not the mathematical one of devising how three can still be one. The problem is the religious one, which Arius raises, of how divinity can be produced and still be divinity. And this is the problem that Athanasius addresses. *If absoluteness is not the de-*

cisive mark *of God's divinity, then what is?* What is the
element of God that should arouse our human worship?
If the Son is generated, but at the same time is just as
divine as the ungenerated Father, then what constitutes
God's divinity?

Athanasius finds the answer explicitly stated in those
passages from the Gospel of John which describe the relations between the Father and the Son. There it is said:
All that the Father has is given to the Son (ch. 16: 15).
As the Father has life in himself, so he has granted the
Son also to have life in himself. (Ch. 5:'26.) Whatever
the Father does the Son does likewise, for the Father
loves the Son and shows him all that he is doing. (Vs.
19 f.) Because the Father loves the Son, he has given
all things into his hand (ch. 3: 35), so that all may honor
the Son as they honor the Father (ch. 5: 23).

On the basis of these passages, then, what is the decisive mark of the Father? It is the *love* by which he
"gives" all things to the Son, including the honor and
reverence due to him as God.

In another set of passages in the Gospel of John, the
Son says of himself: I seek not my own will but the will
of him who sent me (ch. 5: 30). I do nothing on my
own authority, but speak only as the Father has taught
me. (Ch. 8: 28.) All that I do I do so that the Father
may be glorified. (Ch. 14: 13.) Therefore he who believes in me, believes not in me but in him who sent me.
(Ch. 12: 44.)

According to these verses, then, what is the decisive
mark of the Son? It is the *love* by which he yields all
glory back to the Father.

What constitutes the essential mark of God's divinity,

therefore, is love, the bestowing love of the Father for the Son and the adoring love of the Son for the Father.

Let us put the matter another way. Between the Father and the Son there exists a relationship of *total and mutual self-giving.* The Father and the Son are not just entities who contain within themselves a divine level of reality, and who tenaciously hold onto what they have, in the fashion of Arius' God. The Father and the Son have divine reality in *a state of action,* in the action of total self-communication. In fact, Athanasius' point is that this state of action, this act of self-giving is the *essential mark of God's divinity.* The Father and the Son do not have their identity in terms of the reality that they possess and hold onto within themselves, but in terms of their giving this reality to the other. If God's reality in himself is the relation between Father and Son, then God is this staggering dynamism of mutual self-communication. Because the Father holds nothing back but gives all his glory to the Son, and because the Son holds nothing back but offers all that he has to glorify the Father, God within himself is supreme in the order of love.

NEEDY, YET STILL GOD!

Obviously, Athanasius had to reject the notion of God's unity which Arius championed. God, he held, is not a monad, a static, undifferentiated, monolithic "blob." The distinction between the Father and the Son is not external or accidental or temporary. God never existed from all eternity as a solitary being. Always there was the Father generating the Son, and the Son glorifying the Father.

For Athanasius the simple unitarian notion of Arius is too crude a notion for God. God is one, yes, but in a very special sense. The content of his reality is one, because the being of the Son is derived from the Father and therefore possesses no new content. But more important, God's unity is a unity of love, a unity in which the identity of each party is not swallowed up and annihilated but established. Arius' notion of unity is devoid of the richness—and the mystery—of God's unity. It is devoid of the unity of love.

More interestingly, Athanasius points out that any God with the kind of monadic unity and self-sufficient absoluteness that Arius celebrates must be, within himself, an *agonos theos*, a sterile God. Such a God is not generative, not fecund; in short, he must be a dead God. He must be a light that does not shine, a fountain that has gone dry, a barren thing. And if within himself he is such an inert and barren unitarian monad, asks Athanasius, then where does he get the creative power to produce the world?

Finally, Athanasius identifies the dynamic giving between the Father and the Son as the inner life of God, as the life that vitalizes God, not only in all his dealings with his creatures, but also eternally within himself. For that reason Athanasius can insist that generation of the Son by the Father and the adoration of the Father by the Son are not acts done just once, but permanent and eternal *activities* within the being of God. Throughout all eternity the Father is communicating his reality to the

Son; and throughout all eternity the Son is giving all glory to the Father. These are not acts which cause changes in God; they are eternal processes which make up God's essential aliveness.

The issue between Arius and Athanasius, then, has nothing to do with whether God is one or two or three. It has to do with what quality makes God divine, what quality constitutes his perfection. From the perspective of self-contained absoluteness and transcendent supremacy, Arius can only look upon God's begetting a Son as a grotesque blasphemy. God, he observed, must be very imperfect if he must generate a Son in order to become complete. But from the perspective of self-communicating love, Athanasius can look upon the dependent derived Son, not as a blot upon God's divinity, but as a mode of its perfection. Love and not transcendence, giving and not being superior, are the qualities that mark God's divinity.

Since giving entails receiving, there must be a receptive, dependent, needy pole within the being of God. It is pride—and not love—that fears dependence and that worships transcendence. But Arius insists that the Father's divinity requires him to remain superior to the Son and to keep his divine reality exclusively for himself. Arius treats incommunicability—that is, the inability to give and share itself—as the decisive mark of God. In so doing, he is worshiping the very opposite of God.

But we, Athanasius says, believe that the Father is almighty, not because he keeps the Son inferior to himself and uses the Son to display his own superiority, like a Gentile lord, but because he generates the Son as true

God from his own substance and confers all his glory upon the Son.

Therefore, in challenging the whole religious viewpoint of Arius, it was only necessary for Athanasius to insist on one point: the Son, who is generated and derived, who is not sufficient in himself but needy, is still perfect God—God from God, Light from Light, Very God from Very God.

SERVICE, NOT DOMINATION

We noted in Chapter 3 that God exercises his power in Jesus Christ in the mode of service, and not in the mode of domination. The Trinitarian doctrine of the eternal generation of the Son understands this exercise as rooted in God's own nature. Thus, within himself God is a dynamism of giving and receiving, and of needing and serving. We must now ask: *What is God like in his relations to men?*

There can be only one answer. God exercises his power in relation to men through self-giving love and service. There is no possibility that by some fluke God should suddenly decide to suspend this kind of powerfulness and become as a Gentile lord who dominates his creatures with violent power. God has a specific character, a specific kind of powerfulness within himself. He can no more dissociate himself from that mode of power than he can dissociate himself from his own inner reality.

When Jesus stands opposed to all acts of violence and to all violent powers, and when he acts to free men from those forces which oppress and torment them, he does so as the revealer of God's own essential life.

ATHANASIUS AND ARIUS: A STUDY IN CONTRASTS

Let us conclude this chapter by setting the Trinitarian God and the Arian God in the sharpest possible contrast so that all the issues may be clearly seen.

At one level, we are concerned with the question of God's essential being, of the quality that gives him his identity as God. According to Arius, the indispensable mark of divinity is unbegottenness, or what we might call absolute independence. God is divine because he exists wholly from within himself, wholly on his own. He needs nothing, he depends on nothing, he is in essence related to nothing. And this, according to the Trinitarian theologians, is precisely what the powerfulness disclosed in Jesus Christ discredits. For as these theologians read certain passages in the Gospel of John, the powerfulness in Jesus is characterized as fully and perfectly divine, and yet at the same time, as totally and continually derived.

In other words, as present in Jesus, God's powerfulness has a form—the form of dependence—which Arius can only reject as quite unworthy of God. In place of self-contained and self-sufficient autonomy, what the Trinitarian theologians see as the defining mark of divinity is that totality of self-giving which proceeds between the Father and the Son. The Father gives all that he is to the Son; the Son obeys the Father and offers all that he is back to the Father. The Father and the Son are not divine, therefore, in terms of the richness of reality that they possess within themselves. They do not exist closed up within their own being. Rather, they are divine in terms of the richness of the reality that they *communicate to the other.* Against Arius' reverential awe of the absolute, Gregory of Nazianzus puts the alternative:

> Thus much we for our part will be bold to say, that if it is a great thing for the Father to be unoriginate, it is no less a thing for the Son to have been begotten of such a Father. For not only would he share the glory of the unoriginate, since he is of the unoriginate, but he has the added glory of his generation, a thing so great and augúst in the eyes of all those who are not altogether groveling and material in mind. (*Theological Orations* III. 11; *Christology of the Later Fathers,* p. 168.)

If Arius identifies God's divinity with his absolute independence, Gregory identifies it with his inner life of self-giving.

At a second level, we are faced with the question of how God exercises his divinity in relation to the world and to men. For Arius, God's complete self-sufficiency means that with the world he appears in the form of absolute domination. As God depends on nothing, everything else depends on him. As he is completely rich, everything else is completely poor. As he is completely powerful, everything else is completely weak, and is called to revere his power. And as he can affect other things without himself being affected, i.e., through an intermediary agent, everything else in its activity affects itself and other things, but not him.

According to the Trinitarian theologians, nothing could be more contrary to the power of God that men encounter in Jesus Christ than this Arian picture. Far from being a vessel of dominating mastery, Jesus is just the opposite. He does not come on clouds of glory. He does not stand over his followers, ordering them hither

and yon to do his bidding and vindicating his authority
by unopposable acts of self-assertion. In the Epistle to
Diognetus, an early Christian writing, the question is
asked, Why did God send his Son?

To rule as a tyrant, to inspire terror and astonishment? No,
he did not. No, he sent him in gentleness and mildness. To be
sure, as a king sending his royal son, he sent him as God. But
he sent him as to men, as saving and persuading them, and not
as exercising force. For force is no attribute of God.

"Force is no attribute of God"—that is the basic principle for the Trinitarian theologians. God's divinity does
not consist in his ability to push things around, to make
and break, to impose his will from the security of some
heavenly remoteness, and to sit in grandeur while all the
world does his bidding. Far from staying above the
world, he sends his own glory into it. Far from imposing,
he invites and persuades. Far from demanding service
from men in order to enhance himself, he gives his life
in service to men for their enhancement. But God acts
toward the world in this way because within himself he
is a life of self-giving.

5

The Victory of Christ

IN THE previous chapter we considered the depths of God. Is our inquiry now at an end? One might be tempted to stop the investigation at this point. After all, the question of the inner life of God himself seems to be the final subject. The life of God is the crown of all reality. And God is the goal of the Christian life and its ultimate resting place.

But in the present world men have not yet attained this goal. They cannot stand directly and fully within the divine life. As Paul writes, "We know that while we are at home in the body we are away from the Lord." (II Cor. 5: 6.) Evil remains a profound factor in human existence. Men are oriented toward the life and light of God's inner reality only insofar as God frees them from evil and leads them toward himself. But such orientation is incomplete and partial at best. The Christ through whom men are related to eternal life now stands before them as the one who is victoriously overcoming the forces of evil.

And therefore it would be quite mistaken to think that because we have considered the fullness of God, all other problems of faith and life have been taken care of. The knowledge of God's nature, given to us in Jesus Christ, must interact with our earthly experience of evil and its consequences. Christ throws light on the dark side of life precisely because he helps us in becoming liberated from our darkness.

No Two-faced God!

It is possible to speak of "evil" as that which contradicts the good of man. But for the Christian life it is not man but God who determines what evil is. The Bible therefore speaks of evil as that which opposes *God's* will, or as that which mocks *God's* power, or as that which abuses *God's* goodness. If God within himself is an eternal interchange of self-giving between the Father and the Son, we must now try to see why acts that are designed to hurt and cause suffering are essentially evil. It is obvious that such acts contradict the good of man when man is a victim of suffering. But in what sense do they also stand opposed to God?

Violent suffering is the product of excessive power. It shows that one thing is able to dispose of something else, is able to break it and shatter it. It represents, therefore, the decisive way by which any agent can prove that it has power *over* another thing. If God had no character of his own but were simply the bearer of any and every sort of power, if he acted always to vindicate himself at the expense of other things and in that sense were the absolute intensification of all power, then he would have to be honored as the supreme agent of violence. Then all torturing and degradation, all action by which one creature uses his superior power to exploit the weakness of others and to subject them to his control and domination would be an expression of God's kind of power.

But by his life and teachings, Jesus makes perfectly clear that the divinity active through him is *not Absolute Power*. That divinity is not a potentially tyrannical force that might do just anything at all, such as produce square circles or smash the world to pieces. Within himself God is the life and power and energy whereby the Father generates the Son as his perfect equal in all regards and the Son adores the Father as his perfect origin in all regards. Therefore, in his outward actions toward his creatures, God does not act by some other kind of life or power. The energy that informs all his dealings with men is the energy of his own being.

Thus, when God moves toward his creatures, he does not exercise his powerfulness by subjecting them to his domination, or by shattering them with his superior force so as to demonstrate their helplessness before him. The God revealed in Jesus Christ is not brute power raised to the nth degree. This God exercises his powerfulness by his *giving*, by how much he *nourishes* his creatures, by how fully he *communicates* his own reality to them. To be sure, their being lifted by him into life may involve pain to them. But this pain is only a means for their elevation, not an enhancement of God at their expense. Because of his essential nature as the loving community of Father and Son, God *cannot* act without conferring something of himself on those toward whom he acts.

Therefore, should God will that certain creatures dry and shrivel up, losing their vigor and life, he does not attain this by acting upon them positively with violent force, for "force is no attribute of God." He simply *withdraws* his action from them. In these terms, then, a creature's misery and death can only be the result of God's inaction and absence, not of his active presence.

This leads us to a judgment about the behavior of creatures. When they use force to exploit the weakness of others and by this means establish their superiority and domination over others, they are not then acting by the power of God, they are not then being vitalized by the life of God, and they are not then proceeding in accord with the will of God. In short, they belong to the realm of evil. As Jesus said:

"You know that those who are supposed to rule over the Gentiles lord it over them, and their great men exercise authority over them. But it shall not be so among you. . . . For the Son of man . . . came not to be served but to serve, and to give his life as a ransom for many." (Mark 10: 42-45.)

If Jesus is the revelation of the essential power and life of God, then men cannot do violence to one another for their own self-expansion within the area of his Lordship. So far as they do this, they are exercising a powerfulness that contradicts the power of God. They have turned from the light to darkness.

What Is the Source of Ungodly Power?

It has been customary for many Christians to interpret evil chiefly in relation to man. Whenever a person acts in a selfish or cruel way, it is believed, he sets himself outside the sphere of God's love. He then stands forth as the personification of evil in its worst form. He becomes the chief source of ungodly power. From this it is thought to follow that if the human heart could be cleansed of its self-centeredness and if all men would let their conduct be shaped by the spirit of love for others, the Kingdom of God would come on earth.

The New Testament writers, however, do not portray evil in these terms. To be sure, men stand opposed to God when they victimize others for their own advancement, when they oppress the weak instead of caring for them, when they seek to nourish their own lives by the power of domination. And this is especially so if they use something that is peculiarly God's to torment others, as the Pharisees were said to oppress the people by means of God's law. According to the New Testament, however, men themselves are not the primary *source* of this oppressive power, however much they may let it shape their lives. The demons are its source.

Furthermore, as a parody of God's Lordship within the realm of his power, there stands the *diabolos* or the *Satan* or the *poneros* (the "evil one") in the demonic order. In order to call attention to the issue of rule and power, the New Testament portrays the devil with the same imagery it uses of God. It speaks of the devil's power (Acts 26: 18), of the devil's works (I John 3: 8), of the devil's children (v. 10), and even of the devil's synagogue (Rev. 2: 9). For the devil represents evil, not at the level of human act and attitude, but at the level of that decisive powerfulness which may master and determine human acts and attitudes. He constitutes ungodly power at its supreme source, the power that informs every act of cruelty and hate in man and also energizes "the world rulers of this present darkness" and "the hosts of wickedness in the heavenly places" (Eph. 6: 12).

For generations of Christians brought up to think of the world as consisting solely of mind and matter, this language in the New Testament made little sense. Since they identified what is human with the rational mind and everything nonhuman with observable matter, they believed that there could not possibly be any demonic powers in the world that could master man. Serious evil was thought to be located mainly in the human mind, in the form of sin, and these generations of Christians spoke of Christ's work in terms of "saving men from their sins."

Today, however, people have been reawakened to a sense of the terrible forces that can suddenly invade the normal world and produce havoc. They no longer identify their anxieties primarily in terms of what *they* have done wrong as free moral agents, that is, in terms of their sins and their guilt, but in terms of these destructive powers which lie ready to attack them—the automobile accident, the sudden layoff of workers in a factory, the nervous breakdown, the appearance of cancer, the outbreak of war. Modern men, therefore, may be in a position to appreciate New Testament language about the devil and his legions. They may rebel at the thought of giving them personal names or treating them as "spiritual" realities, but they can appreciate the *kind* of evil being represented by these forces.

The Power of Evil Is the Power to Kill

The primary effect of demonic power is to make the agent *superior* over what he acts upon. In contrast to the powerfulness exercised by God the Father in his activity of giving all things to the Son and making the Son his perfect equal, the demonic works to subordinate and subjugate everything else to itself. In its giving and withholding, it seeks to set itself above all other things, to exhibit its own richness in contrast to their poverty. But it is able to attain this goal because of what its power is able to do, namely, to *deprive,* to *dispossess,* to *impoverish,* and ultimately to *kill.* These are the decisive effects by which this power proves itself to be genuinely powerful and to have mastery over things. To the extent that it is really able to take away the life and strength and resources by which something exists, it claims the unqualified homage of that thing. In this connection Jesus remarks how the devil was a murderer from the beginning (John 8:44). The power of domination supremely vindicates itself by its ability to kill.

Since death means the loss of one's identity, demonic power also involves a certain judgment about what constitutes the identity of anything. Identity is what anything must have in order to be genuinely itself and to deserve its own name. The assumption here is that *identity depends upon possession.* A person is real so far as he can draw a line around certain items—his body, his thoughts, his house—and claim them as "his own." Because demonic power is able to crack through this line and to deprive a person of the things that make up his identity, it is really able to kill. Its threat of death carries genuine weight.

In this context, however, there is a condition within things that conspires with the demonic and makes them helpless before its power. This is the condition of *need.*

ss represents a fundamental *flaw* in one's iden-
asic inability to rest securely with those things
which are one's own and which lie inside the line between oneself and the rest of reality. Need forces the
self to become open to the not-self; it requires every
man to come to terms with the threats of demonic
power.

WE ARE AS THE POWER THAT RULES US

The recognition of the demonic puts the whole matter of human evil in a new light, for it means that when
men do wrong, they are not generating some kind of
perverse destruction out of themselves, but are simply
submitting to the power of the evil one. They are not
deciding to do bad acts instead of good acts. They are
deciding that satanic power rules them and their world.
Once they make this judgment, their existence necessarily takes on a certain shape. They live in terms of
what they can possess, what is uniquely and solely their
own. They do everything they can to secure themselves
with this kind of identity. They may try to live wholly
independently. They may try to exercise power over
those around them who threaten to deprive them of
what is theirs. And where they face an overwhelming
power that they cannot handle, they may try to appease
it and win its favor.

From this point of view, men partake of evil whenever they live as if the power of domination had real
power to hurt or bless them. Evil is the man who builds
up treasure for himself, in order to enhance his own life.
Evil is the Gentile king who finds fulfillment by lording
his authority over his people. And evil also are his citi-

zens who honor him and imagine that his kind of power can give them security. All these people, whether they are aware of it or not, are declaring that the kind of power that rules them is that of domination.

The New Testament does not view man's predicament primarily in terms of his good or bad actions. The issue of good and evil does not depend on what kind of power people exercise, but on what kind of power they acknowledge as being exercised over them, on what kind of power they *worship* as ruling their lives and their concrete situations. For this reason, the law of life in the New Testament is not that you shall do good. It is that you shall love the God revealed in Jesus, with all your heart and soul and mind and strength, and shall give allegiance to no form of powerfulness but his. Do this, and your own existence will also be conformed to this kind of power and will become a life of self-expending service. However, if a person submits to the satanic realm, and sees himself in a world in which fulfillment depends on the exercise of dominative power, then such a person simply cannot love in the New Testament sense. It is utterly impossible for him to rest his life in the power of self-expenditure, because he does not consider this to be any sort of power at all.

It should be noted, incidentally, that from this perspective there is no point in leveling an attack against selfishness, or in exhorting people to get busy and help others, for if a person sees himself in a world ruled by God the Father and God the Son, then such a person would naturally not act selfishly. To act for another would, as such, be life for him, that is, a participation in God's kind of life.

On the other hand, if a person sees himself in a world where the satanic reigns, then such a person would be insane to act unselfishly. That is why a merely ethical approach to the condition of selfishness is completely futile. In a world of cancer and bombs, where weakness brings contempt and insignificance brings loneliness, it would be monstrous to be unselfish.

Consequently, whether people serve themselves or serve others is not in their power to choose. This is decided wholly in terms of the kind of world in which they think they live, in terms of the kind of power that they see ruling the roost. The issue lies at the level of the god they worship and not in the kind of person that they may want to be. In New Testament terms, they live or die according to the king that holds them and the kingdom to which they belong.

From this perspective, human life as we usually think of it is shaped by satanic power. When we think of power, we think of the capacity of one thing to exercise control over something else, moving it or changing it or protecting it or destroying it. I hit the ball over the fence. I command my children. I run a business. I hold people's attention or compel people's service. To do so is to have power. Any activity is "powerful" insofar as other things have to be passive and pliable in its presence. By its very nature such power involves an opposition, or chasm, between the agent that enjoys the action and the recipient that is acted upon, between the batter and the baseball, the lecturer and his audience, the master and his slaves.

But this power—this forceful power—is precisely the feature that, in the Epistle to Diognetus, "is no attribute

of God." God's powerfulness is just the opposite. Far
from establishing an opposition between the active
agent and the passive recipient, it has the effect of re-
moving such opposition. God *confers* something of his
own life and activity upon those he touches. He communicates himself to the other. When Jesus says that the
Father has given the Son "power *over*" all flesh, he immediately continues, "so that he may give eternal life"
(John 17: 2). Jesus is the revelation that God's Lordship
and sovereignty do not consist in his domination over
men, but in his giving his own life to them. Most of human existence, at least in its outer appearance, is thus
exposed as belonging to the demonic order. It is necessarily involved in perpetrating violence, not because
people are abnormally cruel, but because of the kind of
power on which they base their existence.

The Power of God in the Suffering of Christ

Redemption in Christ can now mean only one thing:
men are liberated from satanic power and are possessed
by the power of God. In the language of the New Testament they enter "the kingdom of God," the realm where
God's power rules.

In Jesus Christ, God breaks into the domain of Satan
and actually brings men under His Lordship. It is not
the case, then, that throughout all history men have always been directly in the sphere of God's power. God's
power must indeed have undergirded the world and the
human race in all its doings, establishing it with whatever true reality it had. But men have found themselves

cut off from God and apparently enveloped in a universe in which dominative power is lord.

Christ brings the revelation of the power of God. Christ *is* the power of God in victorious action against the pretense of satanic power. In the presence of Christ, dominative power is exposed as impotent, as unworthy of our awe and reverence.

But how does Christ disclose this? In his *death!* Precisely at the point where the demonic should be proving once and for all its control over all things—here over one who claims to be God's Messiah—it is exposed in its hollowness.

For what happens on the cross? In that event the entire energy of the world moves in unison to destroy Jesus and to prove that the power to deprive holds sway. The disciples desert, deny, and betray him. Jesus is whipped and mocked and tortured. In the end he dies. His identity in terms of his possessions is ended. Yet the passion narratives in the Gospels make it perfectly clear that this is not all that is going on. Jesus is not a merely passive victim of brutality. He continues to be active in two ways: he offers all that he is and does to the glory of the Father. "Not my will, but thine be done." (Luke 22:42.) And he continues to expend himself for his brothers in the service of their need. Specifically, he gives himself in service to their need to be shown the impotence of satanic power.

In this particular activity Jesus is the incarnate Son of God. Within God, the Son lives eternally in the act of offering all that he has received back to the Father. The Son's life—or mode of self-communication—is not the same as that of the Father. The Son does not generate, does not produce, does not establish the Father. This generative kind of self-giving is the peculiar mark of the Father. The Son proceeds in a different way: in his self-giving he "offers" himself to the Father.

This is the action, in all its radical fullness, which Jesus exhibits *on the cross*. He does not hang there as a man so securely in possession of certain things that no dominative power can take them from him. Rather, he offers himself to the Father, fully and completely. "Into thy hands I commit my spirit!" (Luke 23:46.)

Jesus here is not simply a creature who, in the face of destitution and death, grovels before God the Almighty, in the hope that this God will not let him be deprived of his own self-contained identity. Jesus' self-offering on the cross and his whole life in Palestine is the action of the Son, and therefore an action in which a human mode of being is gathered into the inner life of God. Here the eternal life of the Son—his life of obedient self-offering to the Father—makes itself present in the flesh of Jesus, and supremely on the cross.

The cross of Jesus Christ tells us that identity with God and identity with the satanic realm are absolutely incompatible. If a man shares in the life of God, his real life will be found in *the act of offering himself in adoration to God,* and in obedience to God, through service to his neighbors. The cross demonstrates that such offering involves a real *letting go* of the self. It involves dispossession, loss of identity *in the satanic terms of possession and identity.*

At the same time, however, Jesus' loss of this identity coincides with the establishing of his identity in the opposing terms, in terms of self-offering to God. What Jesus offers he constantly receives from the Father. And in such offering he is real, not by virtue of receiving and possessing, but by virtue of giving all back to the Father.

Men cannot believe that having an identity within the life of God, an identity of self-offering and self-expenditure, requires their real abandonment of *all* their self-contained identity. They cannot believe that such an identity requires them to will their death, as the world understands death. This is the scandal of the cross. (Luke 17: 33.)

The crucifixion is therefore the most luminous manifestation of the Son's real nature, for there no trace of identity by possession remains. There the power of the satanic is not avoided or blocked. It is allowed to proceed unchecked, so as to be exposed in its total futility. That power seeks to vindicate itself by its ability to threaten—or to shatter—a secure kind of identity. But if the identity that the satanic power seeks to threaten is no real identity at all, then the blessings of ungodly power are sterile and its threats are hollow.

Perhaps that is why the Gospel of John points to the crucifixion as the supreme manifestation of God's power for the men and women of this world. There the Son is glorified and the whole pretense of dominative power is exposed. There the satanic power is decisively brought to judgment. Jesus, speaking of the death by which he was to die, said, "Now is the judgment of this world, now shall the ruler of this world be cast out; and I, when I am lifted up from the earth [upon the cross], will draw all men to myself" (John 12: 31-32).

At this point a warning is necessary. Many people

have been led to think of Jesus' death as the victory of satanic power and therefore to look to the resurrection as the victory of God. After losing the first round to the devil, so to speak, God came back after three days to win the fight.

But in point of fact, the cross does not represent a victory for the Satanic, a proof of its real, decisive powerfulness. And it is not the case that in order to vindicate himself, God had to run away from the world where the devil worked, in order to display his power in some supernatural, resurrected arena inaccessible to the evil one. So genuine is God's power that he was able to vindicate himself even while letting demonic power act to the fullest. In the very process of being killed and deprived of all his possessed identity, Jesus' human being still was never separated from his share in the divine life of self-giving. In this sense, the cross represents the victory of God, and the failure—though not the abolition—of satanic pretense.

What the resurrection adds to the cross is this abolition. For on his return from death, Jesus is portrayed as existing wholly outside the realm where death operates. Dominative power, with all of its pretenses, is here done away with completely. Jesus' concrete human being is irradiated visibly by no power but the power of God. The victory of Jesus' identity in the life of God, which God secures on the cross, is here carried out onto the surface of Jesus' whole existence.

In this present world, the Christian looks forward to the abolition of satanic pretense. But in his day-to-day encounter with the forces of violence, disease and death, he does not hope dreamily for some heavenly South Sea island where everything will be different. He lives now under the cross. He knows that even when it acts most violently, dominative power is not the lord of real life and death. He knows it can only deprive him of the identity that is no real identity, and cannot separate him from his present share in God's life.

No Longer Slaves, but Sons

In Jesus men are saved, not primarily from themselves, but from a whole realm of existence. They are saved from an entire world that is based on dominative power and self-enclosed security. In Paul's phrase, they now become sons of God, not slaves of fear (Rom. 8: 15). For a slave belongs to his master by the power of domination and necessarily obeys out of fear of what that power may do. But in Jesus Christ, Paul asserts, men are not so related to God, "receiving the spirit of slavery and falling back into fear." For that fearful, dominative kind of power does not belong to God. We are related to him as to one who communicates himself. We receive from him his very life, and therefore are his sons and heirs.

So far as men abandon their old identities and become sons of God, they are able to look upon the terrible destructive force of dominative power and not be terrified. As Jesus says, they can be dragged before the Gentile rulers who lord it over people and not be intimidated (Matt. 10: 18). "I have said this to you," he said to his disciples, "that in me you may have peace. In the world you have tribulation; but be of good cheer, I have overcome the world." (John 16: 33.)

6

Resting in Our Need

THE revelation of Christ transforms completely the significance of human need. As long as real power is seen as the capacity to force and dominate, and as long as a person finds his identity in what belongs peculiarly to him and to no one else, then every need that he has represents a threat to his well-being. Need puts a man at the disposal of those people who happen to possess what he requires, and it also represents an aspect of himself in which he lacks anything of his own. For example, anyone who hungers for the love of a particular person may find himself helplessly at the disposal of that person. Since he needs and wants the other's affection, he stands ready to be pushed or pulled as the other may wish. Or again, a person who lacks physical charm can have no identity in that arena, nothing of his own that establishes him amid others.

It is very common for men within the satanic frame of reference to identify need as the great "flaw" in things. Therefore, they picture God as one who lacks this flaw, who has no needs, who stands independently and immutably within the circle of his own identity.

What they feel compelled to remove from their picture of God is that which they most fear and most despair: their condition of need.

When, however, true power is seen as consisting in the exercise of service, in the life of self-giving, and therefore when men find their identity in their serving rather than in their having, then need ceases to be a threat. Instead it becomes the *occasion* and *reason* for service, which is to say, for genuine life. To remove need would be to make the exercise of this kind of power and the enjoyment of this kind of life impossible. Without need there would be no creative and fruit-bearing love in the world.

From this point of view, then, the condition of needlessness that men most admire in the satanic kingdom is actually a condition of utter sterility and death, a condition that makes love unnecessary.

THE LOVELESSNESS OF DECENT PEOPLE

It is very easy for Christians to forget their condition of need and, in a subtle concession to the satanic world, to imagine that in *their loving* they are completely strong. Does not Jesus exhort them to love and therefore, in this regard, does he not identify them with their strength and call them away from all weakness and need? For over a century now the parable of the good Samaritan has been offered as decisive proof for this view. In the face of their needy neighbors, Jesus there directs his followers to be strong and not weak, to be full and not needy, in short, to be totally and unhesitatingly loving.

But we must remember that the parable of the good Samaritan was a response to a question by a lawyer who asked, "Who is my neighbor?" (Luke 10: 29). It is significant that Jesus should answer this question with a parable about traveling, for there is nothing like travel to complicate the question of our neighbor.

Think for a moment of recent developments regarding travel by automobile. There are the wide superhighways, the force of eight-cylinder engines, the ease of power brakes and power steering. These have enhanced travel, not simply for our bodies, but especially for our nerves. All of these help us to keep other persons out of our way. What, for instance, are the great advantages of the superhighways? Because of them we do not have to worry about the people coming toward us from the other direction. We are protected from the delay of towns, from the impudent intrusion of homes, traffic lights, and pedestrians. What is the purpose of our engines with their enormous horsepower? The better to pass people in other cars, to be able to leave them behind, to dismiss and forget them. Why the millions of road signs? So that we can be on our way, without having to stop and ask directions from some other person, and to remember whether he said the third left after the second right, or the second right after the third left.

Now all this is justified because, after all, our time is precious. We have important things to do. We have to get to the station, to the appointment, to the store, to the motel by a certain time. We have only a little while for each of our friends, even less perhaps for our families. The woman who pushes a baby carriage slowly across our way, the dog staring at us quizzically from the middle of the road without moving, the stores and blind intersections—these things drain from us precious time and effort. That is why we encase ourselves in metal and rip along the pavement, protecting ourselves from other people.

With this in mind, one can feel a certain sympathy for the two travelers in Jesus' story who passed by the injured man on the other side of the road. They were the priest and the Levite. In them, of course, we have a reminder of man's inhumanity to man. Therefore it is easy to think of them as cruel, deliberately brutal people. How easy to put anger in our voices when we tell our children about that priest and Levite! How easy—but also how false.

What we forget is that these were persons of responsibility, persons with important projects. Their time and effort had a special significance, for the priest and the Levite were the ones who guided and expressed the desire of the Jewish people to praise the Lord. The Levite instructed the young in the ways of their faith, and helped the adults prepare for their active worship. The priest yielded up to God the offerings and the desires of the people, adoring God with as perfect a sacrifice as possible. Along with these normal functions, there gravitated to these individuals many of the social and political problems of their society.

In good conscience, could these men, caught up in serious responsibilities, turn aside from their schedule to help that single man who had been injured on the road? Must not they hurry on, in the hopes that the next, less busy passerby could give him help? After all, they were not physicians trained to treat the man's injuries. Their work was religious. Their appointed task was to pray and sacrifice for the people. They were called to be the voice even of that injured man in the Temple of the Lord. Can we who tolerate no interference on our way to the beach or to the movie, who want wider highways and faster cars precisely to escape the intrusion of people, condemn the haste of the priest and the Levite? Can we angrily denounce them for deliberate cruelty when we do everything that we can to keep people out of our way with such slogans as "Speed" and "Safety"? Ought we to be shocked at their passing by on the other side of the road, when we put signs along our superhighways which tell our needy neighbor, "If in trouble, get off the pavement!"?

We need not assume, therefore, that it was deliberate cruelty or even selfishness that caused the priest and the Levite to pass by. Their reasons for doing so may very well have been simply the weight of appointments and the tangle of their responsibilities to God and the Jewish community. The problem of neighborly love which faces us in this parable is not to be solved by decent living and ordinary friendliness. Jewish priests were certainly decent enough, as decent as any of us. All that Jesus says in this parable is that the priest and the Levite passed by, whatever their reasons. From the particular viewpoint of the wounded man on the side of the road, they did not have compassion.

THE EXCESSIVE LOVE OF THE SAMARITAN

The fact that these two Jewish officials were not monsters becomes even clearer if we examine the Samaritan. Note carefully the way in which Jesus describes his conduct.

"A Samaritan, as he journeyed, came to where he was; and when he saw him, he had compassion, and went to him and bound up his wounds, pouring on oil and wine; then he set him on his own beast and brought him to an inn, and took care of him. And the next day he took out two denarii and gave them to the innkeeper, saying, 'Take care of him; and whatever more you spend, I will repay you when I come back.'" (Luke 10: 33-35.)

One thing that stands out here is the unlimited character of this Samaritan's service. Jesus emphasizes dramatically that there is apparently no limit to the expenditure that he is willing to make. He pours oil and wine on the man's wounds, stays with him all night, and even accepts responsibility for all future expenses. The story stresses this aspect of the Samaritan's conduct. In that final acceptance of all later expenses, Jesus makes clear that the charity of this man embraces even the future.

The trouble is that we forget exactly what the Samaritan did, how unlimited was his service, how unstinted and single-minded his compassion. We forget his abnormality. We picture him instead as acting in a normal and decent manner. We liken his good deeds to the way in which we might write a check to CARE, or give a pint of blood to the Red Cross, or spend an hour or so a week as a volunteer orderly at the hospital. But these are all things that we *can afford*. We are giving to others what is *not* crucial for ourselves—those few dollars, that surplus pint of blood, that extra bit of time. Our life is not deprived by any of these things. In all of this charity we are being shrewd and cautious about our own needs. And because we think of the good Samaritan's charity in the same way, we do not understand the priest and the Levite at all. They seem abnormal and monstrous.

But this "normal" way of giving is precisely what we do not find in the good Samaritan. At each point in the story, Jesus carefully emphasizes the excessiveness of what the Samaritan does. This man is not acting with sensible caution. "Whatever more you spend, I will repay you when I return," he says. Do many of us have such surplus resources to be able ever to make that statement? Certainly a member of the dispossessed and persecuted Samaritan nation did not.

And that is the point that Jesus drives home. This Samaritan does not love in comfortable accord with his own self-interest. He does not balance his service to the wounded man with a reasonable concern for himself. He seems strangely oblivious about his own needs. If we remember this, we will not be so hard on the priest and the Levite. After all, in failing to act like the good Samaritan, they were simply being normal.

Who Is My Neighbor?

There is a second aspect of the parable that needs reconsideration. What is Jesus trying to tell the lawyer by means of this story? We have the impression that in this story Jesus is trying to show us *how* we should go about loving our neighbor. He is trying to explain what it means in practice for us to be Christians and to serve others. He is trying to teach us how to be a neighbor to other people. Certainly all these are involved. After presenting the Samaritan to us, Jesus does say, "Go and do likewise." But that is not the primary point of his story, and neither is it the primary problem in everyday life.

In reading the parable in this way, we forget what it is that causes Jesus to tell his story. In other words, we forget the lawyer and the lawyer's question. Now the lawyer did not ask Jesus: How do I love my neighbor? How do I go about fulfilling God's command? What should *I* do to be a neighbor to others? The lawyer asks: *Who is my neighbor?* Whom should I love? Where can I find someone—anyone—who will prove himself a neighbor to me, so that I may love him?

In other words, upon being confronted by God's command "to love your neighbor as yourself," the young lawyer asks just what you and I ask every day: Who is such a neighbor to me that I should love him as myself? I know the people around me—priests and Levites who are caught up in their lofty responsibilities, shopkeepers who give me dubious goods, doctors who burden me with heavy fees, politicians who siphon off my money, negligent husbands who are caught up in their work, and anxious wives who take all the zest and danger and excitement out of life. We all know these people because we all know ourselves. Everything in them is present in us too—self-importance, deceit, greed, and cowardice. We are not perplexed about *how* to love our neighbor. The suffering and the anguish in the world are obvious enough to call forth a charitable response. We do not need Jesus' story to remind us of that.

Our trouble is the one that bothers the lawyer. We can never find anyone who awakens our love. We can never find anyone who, however much he does for us, is not also looking out for himself, at least to a reasonable extent. Our difficulty is not that we are full of love, and only need a little guidance from Jesus as to how we may best exercise it. Our difficulty is that we have no love, and we have no love because we have no true neighbor, no one who, in Jesus' words, proves to be a neighbor to us. We know human nature too well to be deceived by appearances. If God commands us to love our neighbor, where do we find him?

That is the lawyer's question. It is everyone's question. For men begin in need and not in love. And that is the question that Jesus answers with his parable—not how, but *whom,* do I love? Not, How can I be a neighbor to others? but, *Who* is a neighbor to me? Jesus tells his story of how three different people—a priest, a Levite, and a Samaritan—act toward the wounded man. In conclusion he asks, Which of these three proved to be a neighbor to that wounded man? That is, Which of these three does God command the wounded man to love?

In other words, in this conclusion Jesus simply repeats the lawyer's original question in terms of his own story —not, "Who is my neighbor?" but, "Who is the neighbor to the wounded man?" And the lawyer gives the answer: "The one who had compassion," the Samaritan.

It seems, then, according to Jesus, that when God commands us to love our neighbor, that neighbor is not just anybody, and is certainly not a half-dead needy person on the side of the road. Our neighbor is the one who "proves" to be a neighbor, the one who is compassionate to us, the one who picks us up and pours oil and wine on our wounds, who takes us to an inn and stays with us all night, and who assumes complete responsibility for any expense that we may have in the future for our recovery. According to Jesus in this parable, that is the neighbor whom God commands us to love as ourselves.

WHO IS THE GOOD SAMARITAN?

We no sooner read the parable in this way than we seem to be faced with an insuperable problem. If the neighbor whom God commands us to love is someone who acts like a good Samaritan, where can we find him? Certainly not among the priests and Levites of this world. The story itself is careful to indicate that. And certainly not among the real Samaritans living north of Jerusalem. They are poor and dispossessed. Having undertaken a rather realistic analysis of the problem of the man of responsibility, the priest or the Levite, we must not be too romantic about the poor. If the priest and the Levite are burdened by their serious duties, the poor are burdened by envy and spite and self-pity. It is not the case that we have only to move forty miles north of Jerusalem and, behold, there among the real Samaritans we will find a good Samaritan.

It seems, in other words, that the lawyer is justified in his question. If this story is meant to describe the neighbor whom God commands him to love, then he can only conclude that he has no such neighbor. Has Jesus given us only some make-believe in this figure of the good Samaritan? Does a neighbor only exist for us in a story, as an ideal that we imagine in our minds—an ideal of the attentive husband and self-sacrificing wife, an ideal of the perfect ruler, an ideal of the good Samaritan?

As a way through this problem, we must remember once more that this is one of Jesus' parables. The parables are stories that Jesus tells to indicate something of the Kingdom of God which comes *through him*. The parable of the mustard seed: the Kingdom grows overnight. The parable of the laborers in the vineyard: people are gathered into the Kingdom, whether they work a short time or a long time. There is the parable of the lord who sends his son to a country where the people beat and kill him. Jesus' own suffering and rejection as the bearer of the news of the Kingdom is portrayed here. And so with the other parables. Now the story of the good Samaritan is also a parable about the Kingdom of God coming in Jesus Christ. If we look carefully at some of the features of the good Samaritan, we may detect its meaning in relation to Jesus and the Kingdom.

First, who comes to man with help, but comes in a form that is offensive, so offensive in fact that he, like the Samaritan, is a persecuted man and has nowhere to lay his head?

Secondly, who, like this Samaritan, loves others even while being persecuted by them? Who, like the man in the parable, really has compassion and cries, "Father, forgive them for they know not what they do"?

Thirdly, whose love is powerful enough in the perspective of the New Testament not just to sympathize but to bind up wounds and to heal? Who pours oil on man's wounds? Who is the only one able to take responsibility for *all* the care that men need and to protect them from *all* the dangers that they face?

Fourthly, who alone has accepted the full responsibility for men's future, for everything they do from now until the end of time? In the New Testament who is going to "come again," and when he comes again will repay all our debts?

And finally, who is put before us in the New Testament as the only example for us to follow, to go and do likewise? Who says, "I am the way, and the truth, and the life"? Who fulfills the law of love, that we should love our neighbor as ourselves, and fulfills it so perfectly that we see the lovelessness in all the priests and Levites of every nation and every age?

The good Samaritan is Jesus Christ. This story is indeed a parable. Like all Jesus' other parables, it does not tell us about our human love and about how we can go about displaying it to needy people. It tells us about God's love for us in Jesus Christ. It requires us to identify ourselves, not with the heroic Samaritan, but with the poor wounded man on the side of the road. It reminds us that the one who truly serves us and is our neighbor, who saves our life and therefore draws forth our love, does not wear a very reassuring appearance. He does not come with all the badges and character recommendations that we expect. He does not come with charity shining conspicuously all over him. He does not come as a priest or a Levite. The parable warns us, not of the difficulty we face in trying to love others, but of the difficulty that all of us will have in appreciating the one who loves us and lays down his life for us, namely, our neighbor Jesus Christ. Jesus alone is our true neighbor. He comes to us as a Samaritan might come to a Jew. On the surface he is simply not impressive enough to satisfy us. And yet he heals our deepest wounds and brings us the gift of eternal life. From the world's viewpoint, he comes in a broken and contemptible form, apparently incapable even of preserving himself. He is not powerful in terms of his title and function, as is the priest and the Levite, or the chairman of the United Fund or the director of the Red Cross. He is only powerful—but supremely powerful—in the life that he gives to men, healing their human sickness and opening to them the gates of paradise. He so fully restores them that they are enabled to become his servants, and in his name may be compassionate to others as he has been to them. He so heals men that by his power they too can go and do likewise. They too can be a neighbor to others in his name.

The fact that we may be neighbors to one another, however, is only the consequence of the fundamental fact that God himself has given Jesus Christ as our neighbor. The lawyer's question has been answered. Who is my neighbor that I should love him as myself? The good Samaritan, Jesus Christ. Christ is the one whom men are commanded to love. He is the life giver, he who now comes to us under the life-giving forms of bread and wine.

In the light of his service, he is also the one whom men can love easily, naturally, and spontaneously. And even the priest and the Levite must be included here. We are not to think of them as abnormally cruel. They are not Samaritans, to be sure, but the good Samaritan may come even to them and may make them like himself. They are not villains but broken wounded men also, who are not yet aware of their need and who therefore are not ready to receive the good Samaritan. Let us include them not in our charity but in our Lord's charity, for in them it is we who are being represented.

7

Love and Suffering

VIOLENT suffering, which has been the subject of our theological investigation, has proved to be only the upper visible portion of an enormous iceberg. In raising the whole question of power, its sources and effects, we have been led deeply into four major areas of exploration.

1. We have considered the doctrine of God. (What is the nature of the power that God possesses within himself?)

2. We have dealt with the doctrine of evil. (What is the satanic power which for the New Testament represents the supreme form of evil, and how is this power related to human sin?)

3. We have examined the doctrine of redemption. (How is Christ to be understood as the one who liberates the world from this evil power?)

4. And we have devoted attention to the doctrine of man. (What becomes of human neediness under God's power?)

We must now return to the particular theme with which we began our study and inquire about the place of actual suffering in the Christian life.

LOVING IN OUR NEED

We face a temptation when we identify love with the power of God, and speak of service as fulfillment. For when we use these words, we may simply be thinking of love in terms of dominative power. We may, in effect, be imagining that just by loving in Christ's name we may secure precisely those blessings which are usually denied us: namely, a secure identity for ourselves, and a mode of action that is effective in giving us some importance in relation to other people. We are thus tempted to treat love as another strategy in the realm of satanic power.

Such a view is impossible, however, if we remember that our loving, at least when it has the form of service, always means our *dispossession*. It always involves our surrendering to another something of our own, something that secures our old identity as self-contained beings. No sleight of hand is possible here. He who is gathered into the life of God in Christ will be called upon to give to others what he possesses, in order to live by virtue of what possesses him: the life of God.

In relation to this life of service, then, men not only begin in the condition of need but they also *end* in the condition of need. If they are taken to an inn and restored to health by the Good Samaritan, it is only in order that they may then go on to live by expending themselves for others.

The Christian serves the needy neighbor, not as a strategy in the expansion of the self, but as the proper way of fulfilling his being in God. But to live in this way, a person must really disbelieve in dominative power and in the enclosed kind of identity that belongs to such an orientation. He must not be afraid of his needs. He must not hold back from being exposed to the onslaughts of the world, even when he knows that he has nothing of "his own" to fall back on. He must believe in the power of God against all other powers. The life of service is always a deprivation, and therefore a loss of identity in the world's terms. In this special sense, it always involves a willingness to die in the way in which the world understands death, a willingness not to exist by virtue of possessing something that is exclusively one's own. Every act of loving thrusts a person into this crisis of identity, and there is no escape from this peculiar kind of tension.

THE WORLD REACTS

The instant a person renounces his self-enclosed identity and repudiates the power of domination as his lord, he provokes the world against him. He stands as an offense to the world, as a fanatic or a fool. He is not terrified at the prospect of dispossession. He does not seek self-aggrandizement. And therefore nothing can control or master him by threatening to exploit his weaknesses with dominative power. He lives as a witness to another kind of power, to another lord. The world therefore finds him puzzling and dangerous. Something must be done to expose his folly, to show that the power on which he relies is quite impotent.

The Christian thus discovers that the world reacts to him by trying to inflict pain or death upon him. In addition to all the external and internal pains to which he is subject as a man along with other men, the Christian experiences this additional violence precisely and solely because he is a Christian.

Here, too, the Christian feels no final fear. It is not his real identity that is being threatened. Indeed, such suffering is an aspect of his real identity. So far as a person moves toward others by the power of God, he must expect this affliction. He should glory in it, says Paul, because it is a sign of his share in the life of God. And Jesus himself taught his disciples: "Blessed are those who are persecuted for righteousness' sake, for theirs is the kingdom [that is, the share in the power] of heaven" (Matt. 5: 10).

Christians may rejoice because so far as they bear affliction they are sharing in Christ's sufferings and taking up his cross (Mark 8: 34). Again, in the words of Paul, we are "fellow heirs with Christ, provided we suffer with him in order that we may also be glorified with him" (Rom. 8: 17).

THE CHRISTIAN AND SORROW

At the same time it must be emphasized that the Christian has no desire for suffering as such. He does not wish to see himself disturbed or broken by violent power. Strictly speaking, he glories not in his affliction but in his participation in the life of God, of which the world's resentment is only a sign. To glory in suffering for its own sake is really to give homage to the power that does violence.

This brings us to an aspect of the Christian life not often emphasized in our churches today, the element of

Christian sorrow. Too often it has been assumed that the person of faith lives with a kind of perpetual smile on his lips. Faith means an upbeat frame of mind. Of course, this is not true, and nothing either in the New Testament or in Christian experience could justify such an attitude. The Christian rejoices with those who rejoice, but he also weeps with those who weep. (Rom. 12: 15.) He is called, not simply to notice those who suffer and to sympathize with them, but to recognize his own identity with them in their pain and in the deceptions about power in which they are entangled. In short, the Christian has no secure and happy vantage point from which to view sorrow and pain.

In the present world God does not relate us to himself in such a way that we are cut off from our suffering neighbors. God does not so fill the Christian with truth and peace and joy that he may look upon human misery as something from another world. As Christians we know how terrible and degrading is the anguish of bodily pain, of social rejection, of the silence of God. And Christians know how deeply the pretense of violent dominative power can deceive their own hearts and suddenly reclaim their worship. They also know that God's grace is moving them toward a world from which the demonic will have completely vanished. Precisely because they are on the way toward that world and have not yet arrived, they still live in the old world of self-enclosed security and fear and death. Their own existence reflects both the struggle and the victory of Christ. Again and again the darkness that holds them is broken through by Christ's light. Fear is turned into confidence, self-enclosedness turns into self-giving. The worship of dominative power turns into the worship of the power of God. But this happens to the Christian anew each day. For he is asked to live, not for his own happiness, but as the servant of his God to those still in bondage. Therefore he is placed with others in their bondage, so that in him they may see that bondage broken.

The Christian remains fully aware, from his own experience, of ungodly power. Therefore he cannot "enjoy" suffering, as though he were immune to its pains. At the same time he cannot dismiss it, as if it had no importance for his neighbors. And finally, he cannot fear it as the final reality of his existence, since he sees himself —and his neighbors, including his enemies—as under the power of Christ. His attitude toward ungodly power is therefore one of sorrow.

Sorrow comes when we experience the violation of some good. But the Christian does not treat this violation as the first word and last truth about life. If he did that, his sorrow would turn into hate or despair. He knows that he and his loved ones are caught in the violence and deception of brutal power. He does not evade this fact. He sorrows. But he knows that the power that breeds such misery is now being exposed in its pretense, and that the sufferings of this present age are not worth comparing to the glory which God shall reveal (Rom. 8: 18). Therefore, he rejoices. The Christian can know joy in connection with sorrow, but only because he knows the power of God is overcoming the power of evil.

As Christians, then, we must not gloss over the negative element of sorrow and pain with the notion that joy is the single, all-embracing mood of the Christian life.

The joy of life in Christ is a consolation for our sorrow as human beings; it does not remove that sorrow. In the words of Paul:

"Blessed be the God and Father of our Lord Jesus Christ, the Father of mercies and God of all comfort, who comforts us in all our affliction, so that we may be able to comfort those who are in any affliction, with the comfort with which we ourselves are comforted by God." (II Cor. 1: 3-4.)

In God *Alone* We Trust

Yet for the Christian the setting for this feeling of sorrow is his *faith*. From first to last he lives with absolute confidence in the power of God. In this world that means a conscious repudiation of dominative power. But every act of service always involves some measure of deprivation to himself. And the Christian's service never succeeds—and never means to succeed—in freeing others entirely from their needs and weaknesses.

In his need as well as in his service, the Christian must always affirm the opening statement of the Apostles' Creed: "I believe in God the Father Almighty." The almightiness affirmed here is not that of a transcendent God whose power consists in standing above the Son in some kind of superiority. It is not the almightiness of a God who dominates the universe, compels its obedience, and proves his supremacy by always getting his own way. The almightiness affirmed here is that of the Father, which means that it is the almightiness of the one who confers all his own being and glory upon his Son.

To confess that "I believe in God the *Father* Almighty," therefore, is to confess that I believe in the almighty powerfulness of God's self-communication and self-giving. It means that I renounce all awe and admiration for that which merely dominates. By this confession the Christian continues to serve in the face of affliction, until the time comes when the pretenses of demonic power are swept away.

8

A Postscript
on Theological Method

Now, after this brief inquiry into the question of suffering, we must return to the matter of "theological method" which we raised in Chapter 1. What are the procedures for focusing the light of God's revelation upon the situation of human suffering?

First of all, we can say specifically what a theological method is not. It is not a predetermined sequence of steps through which any problem may be carried and which will then of itself produce the correct answer. The human mind in its work of analysis and synthesis, of penetrative insight and creative association—this is what receives the light of God's revelation. Method is no substitute for the labor, the inventiveness, and the risks of reflection. If a person believes that the gospel is not for us men in our actual human being, if he considers that he has some special incompetence which excuses him from joyfully and gratefully receiving its light in a rational way through discourse with his neighbors, and if he imagines that some theological method will then deliver the truth to him ready-made, he is mistaken. No method will give him what he has forfeited by his despair and sloth.

Neither does a theological method lay out some fixed path which the mind may follow in order to secure the truth for its own use. This would be to reduce God's gift of revelation to a humanly controlled legalism. We can no more seize for ourselves the truth of the gospel by making just the right intellectual moves as determined by some law than we can seize holiness for ourselves by conforming our moral decisions to the requirements of some law. Knowledge of God and of ourselves in relation to God is as much an event of his mercy as is the gift of his love. In fact, what else is his love but his opening himself to us and for us. We can await and receive and share insights into the gospel, but we cannot move ourselves to them. They are given, not taken. A theological method may describe the situation in which we stand and the route along which we are carried by God's bestowal of saving knowledge into our darkened minds. But this method does not give us any control over the light of the gospel, and does not enable us to turn on that light whenever we wish.

These two misconceptions of theological method—that it saves us the trouble of thinking or that it gives our thinking a technique to grasp God's truth—are fairly widespread. And both reflect the same fundamental error: they do not take the attainment of knowledge seriously enough. On the one side they tend to locate the work and processes of thinking in some detached realm outside of life. Reasoning, they seem to say, goes on in a strange world of abstract ideas and technical expertness and implacable logic, but does not really count until it has been made "practical," until it has been brought in touch with man's concrete needs and hopes. On the other side, these misconceptions seem to assume that thinking about God's love is not itself a share in God's love but is only a preliminary activity, something done only in order to get on to some other place of personal worship and real confrontation.

Yet surely this is not the case. Christian theology is not a detached, purely theoretical abstraction, which has somehow to be made practical. It itself is the voice of man's actual existence in movement from darkness toward the light. We cannot treat the ignorance and confusions of our rational minds as merely preliminary problems, which if once solved, still leave us unfructified by the gospel. They are an essential part of the evil from which Christ redeems us. Coming to an understanding —a coherent understanding that can be shared with others—of God's work in Christ is as such a share in his life. For the questions investigated by theology, such as the question of suffering considered above, are not intellectual questions, devised by the mind out of its own imperial curiosity. They are the questions of our existence, they are *our existence itself in its questionableness.* That is why the discovery of light by means of our reason in these matters belongs to the very heart of our fellowship with God. However technical its language or abstract its concepts, theology should never have to be made "relevant." From beginning to end it is embedded in the most relevant process in the world: God's transfiguration of human existence.

The Conditions of Our Quest

If a theological method is not some tested procedure for producing answers to theological questions, if it is not a substitute or a law for the mind's creative engagement with the gospel, what is it? A theological method tells us the *conditions* within which the event of understanding seems likely to occur (though not necessarily and not automatically). It indicates where the theologian should be—or may be—what he should be looking at and preoccupied with for the sparks to fly. The method used in this study of suffering has involved two conditions, which marked out the areas where the give-and-take of thinking has occurred.

1. The theologian stands before a real question of human existence, a problem or agony in which the questionable character of life stands fully exposed. It is a matter that he and his world find urgent and shaking. In moving toward a clear grasp of this question, he has open to him the whole fabric of concrete life—the most sensitive artistic expressions, the best scientific generalizations, the boldest philosophic insights, or even, as in Chapter 2, the daily newspapers. These do not serve to give him any answer, for the answer he seeks—and expects—is the reality of God himself. But they do help him to see more clearly the scope and depth and shape of the question at hand. They keep him mindful that he stands in the midst of life and not in a detached thought realm, that he is undertaking a responsible approach to existential and not academic questions.

Not all theology proceeds in terms of some gripping human problem. Biblical theology wrestles with the riches and obscurities of the Scriptural text. Dogmatic theology elaborates the content of the Christian revelation and in that light assesses what is said in various times and by various people about God and man. By virtue of its preoccupation, then, the theological inquiry that we have undertaken might be called problematic or existential or redemptive theology. It consciously seeks the light of Christ in terms of a specific problem of human existence, in the confident expectation that his presence and work will transfigure this problem.

2. A second condition for the theology that we have pursued is for this problem to be brought within the circle of Jesus Christ. But Jesus Christ is not just the answer, not just the truth and the life. He is also the way. We do not have contact with him only on the far side of our confusion and perplexity, as if these were reproachful evils which we have to escape before he will have anything to do with us. He embraces our human predicament within himself, so that in him our questions and torments attain a momentum that moves us into the life of God. In his work of redemption he deepens and intensifies the questionableness of our human existence, because he grounds our life in God, rather than in anything which we possess within ourselves. The existential problem on which a theological inquiry focuses itself constitutes the point where the light of Christ breaks through and where men may understand anew God's goodness to them.

At this point, however, we must distinguish clearly between receiving and giving instruction. Since we are seeking to be instructed, nothing would be gained by referring our problem to some ideas about Christ that had already been produced by our theologizing. Then we would not be receiving instruction for ourselves with regard to the problem at hand, but would be simply using that problem as the occasion to instruct others about our views of Christ. Therefore, in the pages above, it is not to some church's or some theologian's notion as such that we have referred the problem of suffering, but to the witness of the Bible, from which all theological notions receive their life and by which also they must be continually judged. For theology the process of bringing a problem within the circle of Christ's light means to bring it to the witness of the Bible, for that is where Christ presents himself to us.

There is one precise point to be kept in mind while reading the Bible in a theological inquiry. What we seek is a knowledge of God and of the life—the life of glory —to which God is drawing us. We are seeking something that is revealed through, but that lies beyond the confines of, ancient Israel or first-century Palestine. Therefore, when we read the surface words of individual passages in the Bible, and when we learn what we can about their specific meanings and about the circumstances that caused them to be written, we do not stop there. We go beyond this level to the witness that each passage gives to God's eternal graciousness toward men. Therefore we read the words with the utmost care: we are guided by the scholarly studies of the Greek and Hebrew language. We realize that no passage of Scripture was written with us in mind. None stands suspended in some timeless realm, as if so formulated by its author that it could immediately address all future humanity. Every sentence is embedded in a concrete historical situation, and what it says is expressed in the terms of its time. And that is as true of Jesus' teachings as of Paul's discussion of a troublemaker in the church at Corinth. Therefore, everything that the historian can responsibly tell us is important. But it is not Paul's theology, it is not the church in Corinth nor the shape of the gospel within the mental framework of a first-century Palestinian that finally interests us. The concrete historical existence of these people in their encounter with grace itself points beyond their particular encounter to Christ as God's presence and grace for all men, including us. The situation that the historian discovers from the words is itself only a word, opened by God's light so that it points beyond itself to him. In theologizing we cannot do without the text of the Bible or without the historical situations disclosed there, but we receive these as words where God makes himself known to us as our God, as our God now and forever.

To be a witness in this way, Biblical statements do not have to be true in every respect. They are not required to be literal factual reports. They can be poetic and mythic; they can report untrue facts and can reflect widely held misconceptions. The fact that there is no kingdom of death in "the lower parts of the earth," which some geologist may soon discover (Eph. 4: 9), or the fact that no star came so close to the earth that at the time of Jesus' birth it was directly overhead only at Bethlehem (Matt. 2: 9)—such factual "errors" do not deprive these passages of their power to witness.

The Bible is not an infallible interpretation, either in its words or in its presentation of events. It is not the revelation of God: Christ is. But the fact that it points beyond itself to Christ means that it *lets itself*—its words and situations—*be interpreted by him*. It does not assert itself as the truth. In pursuing theology, we enter into that work of interpretation. This, however, is not *our* interpretation, not the process of illuminating Scripture with whatever light we can generate out of our minds. It is the reality of God in Christ which interprets both the words and circumstances of the Bible. Our interpretative work is simply our effort to participate in, to respond to, God's interpretation.

That is why we must always be ready to hear the witness of Scripture in fresh ways, why we cannot demand that it always confirm the beliefs that we had yesterday. Yet because we may be victims of sloth or may deceive ourselves with our own fancies, we seek out the assistance of our neighbors. We let them help us hear the witness of Scripture in fresh ways. In Chapter 4, Athanasius' doctrine of the Son was explored, not because every Christian is slavishly bound to that bishop's thought, but because his thought draws out the Scriptural witness to the power of God with fresh clarity.

The role of faith in theology appears precisely at this point. Faith does not consist in clinging to some catalog of answers that are provided in a catechism. Faith is man's hunger and eagerness for the God who gives himself in Christ. In theology it therefore expresses itself as the reach of a person's mind beyond the words and historical situations of the Bible toward God himself. It is his confident expectation, his demand in fact that every text of Scripture speak to him of this final truth. He refuses to rest in anything less. Like Jacob with the angel, the Christian who theologizes keeps wrestling with a text, coming back to it again and again, until it blesses him. The man without faith may tell us about the meaning of Biblical words or may discover new aspects of the circumstances surrounding Biblical statements, but he cannot share with us this reading of Scripture as the witness of God's Lordship over us.

THE UNENDING NATURE OF OUR QUEST

All theology is provisional. It is the movement of men from darkness toward the light, so that as movement no point along its way has permanent or final validity. Every attainment of understanding soon finds itself confronting new perplexities, and thus called to new investigations.

The exploration of suffering which we have just undertaken probably opens more questions than it resolves. But there are four in particular that deserve attention.

1. Can any theology give priority to the demonic rather than to sin in the order of evil? Is not an understanding of sin one of the great insights of the Protestant Reformers, and while no one is bound to these figures from the past, do they not reflect the Biblical perspective? To insist that evil finds its central form in pretentious powers may be just another strategy by which men minimize their own responsibility.

2. In focusing the whole discussion of God in terms of the relations between the Father and the Son, no mention was made of the Holy Spirit. And while for the New Testament the Spirit has a minor place in comparison with the other two divine persons, it cannot be ignored. What is the nature of the Spirit, within God's own being first, but also in the work of human redemption? And what light does it throw on the suffering of men?

3. In construing the world as now a place where de-

monic pretensions are being unmasked but not yet removed, has there been enough appreciation of the goodness of the present world, of its amenability to human labor and its resilience to human aspiration? Does not the sense of a radical tension at the superhuman level undercut all short-range goals? Is life now only a matter of meeting needs and of opposing their exploitation again and again each day, without any real improvements, without any progressive liberation from need itself? Is man's drive for security within his worldly and social relationships really a matter of denying the Lordship of God? Does Christ do nothing but impose upon us a terrible tension, an either/or alternative? Does he not enable us to dance and to enjoy the casual fun of daily life, without the burden of cosmic convulsions?

4. Finally, for all its theological refinement, does not this perspective finally desert men at the point of utmost importance: the real issues of concrete life. For these the constant problem is not the dismissal of, but the use of, violent destructive power. It is not a matter of lying down before violence, but of applying the energy of violence in a constructive way, to protect the weak or to isolate the criminal. To say that dominative power is a merely pretentious and finally impotent form of power is to speak irrelevantly to everyone but a few saints.

Such are four questions that demand consideration. Should anyone wish to continue this theological inquiry, however, let him proceed under the solicitude of the lovely prayer in Ephesians:

"I bow my knee before the Father, . . . that according to the riches of his glory he may grant you to be strengthened with might through his Spirit in the inner man, and that Christ may dwell in your hearts through faith; that you, being rooted and grounded in love, may have power to comprehend with all the saints what is the breadth and length and height and depth, and to know the love of Christ which surpasses knowledge, that you may be filled with all the fulness of God." (Eph. 3: 14-19.)

65349